RULES AND INSTITUTIONS

RULES
AND
INSTITUTIONS

Nicholas Rowe

THE UNIVERSITY OF MICHIGAN PRESS
Ann Arbor

First published in the United States of America by
The University of Michigan Press 1989

First published 1989 by
Philip Allan
Hemel Hempstead, Hertfordshire, England

Printed and bound in Great Britain

1992   1991   1990   1989   4   3   2   1

Library of Congress Cataloging-in-Publication Data

Rowe, Nicholas, 1955–
    Rules and institutions / Nicholas Rowe.
       p.   cm.
    Bibliography: p.
    Includes index.
    ISBN 0–472–10155–2
    1. Social interaction.   2. Social institutions.   I. Title.
       HM291.R69   1989
       302—dc20   89–5161
                                                        CIP

Contents

Preface

The origins of this book go back to the 1970s. As an undergraduate student majoring in philosophy at Stirling University, I slowly learned that my initial act-utilitarianism was untenable as an ethical doctrine, being unable to give any account, for instance, of things like rights and duties, which seemed to be morally important. Rule-utilitarianism seemed a more promising alternative, and, in principle, able to give an account of the rights and obligations attaching to particular institutions, but the exact distinction between act- and rule-utilitarianism seemed as unclear as the reason for rules. Constrained maximization should either result in a lower value for the maximand than unconstrained maximization, or else the constraint is non-binding. How can it ever be better to follow a rule which requires any actions other than those that are best?

On completing my BA, I switched into economics, and so shelved problems in moral philosophy, until I discovered exactly the same problem reappearing under a different guise. Studying monetary theory, I was trying to make sense of the notion of trust in the social institution of money, and realized that it was not at all clear how one could make sense of *any* social institution using the standard concepts of neoclassical economics, and yet neoclassical economic analysis is nearly always conducted within a given framework of social institutions. (I later realized that most sociologists had recognized this long before, and this was perhaps why they were sociologists and not neoclassical economists, but being a neoclassical economist myself I wasn't going to give up that easily!)

The central question was the ontological one: what sort of stuff were social institutions made of? What sort of thing exists when a social institution exists? They could not be part of the physical environment, like rocks and plants, nor any belief about the natural environment, like the laws of physics. Though 'institutional constraints' could be imposed on human behaviour just like the physical constraints imposed by natural resources and technology, such a fiction could not explain the institutional constraints themselves. Neither could social institutions be part of human preferences — 'people make and obey laws because they like making and obeying them'. Though we could simply assume taboos against lying, stealing and cheating, we would not be explaining where these taboos come from, and why different societies have different taboos. But if social institutions are neither technology nor preferences, what are they? To treat institutions as *sui generis*, so that human action depends on a triad of tastes, technology and institutions, is simply to admit defeat. Better to maintain the dualism of technology and preferences, and say that social institutions are themselves actions, or beliefs about actions. Society is what people do, and expect each other to do. But not every sort of action constitutes an institution. Robinson Crusoe, for instance, acts, but has no social institutions. Again, the idea of following a rule of action seemed important, just as it had seemed important in moral philosophy, but how exactly did following a rule of action differ from simply performing a sequence of actions?

Reading Kydland and Prescott's (1977) paper '*Rules rather than discretion: the inconsistency of optimal plans*' gave the answer I needed — to follow a rule means to *precommit* one's future actions. Imposing the constraint of prior commitments on an agent's choice of action need not lower, but can instead raise his utility: for imposing the constraint paradoxically grants him the freedom to influence other agents' expectations of his future actions, and thus influence their actions.

Though I now had a distinction between rules and actions, together with a reason for rules, the question I wanted to answer had now changed from the normative question of why people *ought* to obey institutional obligations to the positive question of why they *do in fact* (usually) obey them. Though political philosophers, like Rawls (1971) and Nozick (1974) for instance, may use the same analytical devices like the State of Nature, and also stress the importance of rules, they are using them for a different purpose. Interestingly, Hodgson (1967) would seem to have a clear statement of the time-inconsistency problem when he attacks act-utilitarianism on the grounds that '. . . certain good consequences depend on the existence of *expectations* of actions, and that, under certain conditions as to knowledge and rationality, an agent's avowedly acting upon the act-utilitarian principle could preclude such expectations and such good consequences' (ibid, p. 85, emphasis in original). Unfortunately, Hodgson's examples are all set in a world where all agents are act-utilitarians and so perfectly altruistic (each caring about the other's welfare equally to his own), and as I show in Chapter 7, in such contexts the time-inconsistency problem can only arise in a very weak sense — the sense in which the problem can be resolved by a convention, like all driving on the right, which none would *wish* to break. The true time-inconsistency problem only has relevance for an ethics of the 'second best' — how one ought to act when not all others are acting as they ought. For the world of 'homo economicus', of course, the world is always 'second best' in this sense, for each selfish agent invariably finds that other selfish agents do not act in a way that would serve *him* best, and so the time-inconsistency problem is almost always relevant, and so he follows rules, and observes and expects others to do so too, and his world becomes a social world.

These ideas have been gestating since my first introduction to philosophy. It has taken me a very long time to get my thoughts even as straight as they are now. Just to understand what question I was trying to answer was not at all clear until long after I had tried to answer it. But it was (usually) fun. I entered and leave this topic as a macroeconomist; but to have done true justice to it I would need to be fully proficient, not only in many other areas of economics, but also in philosophy, sociology, game-theory, political science, and perhaps others. I can only apologize to all those whose work I should have read and cited but have not.

Acknowledgements

This material has gone through so many metamorphoses since its original inception that some who commented on earlier versions of various parts may not recognize the final result. I thank them for their help, whether or not I adopted all their suggestions or answered all their criticisms.

My main debt is to David Laidler. Quite apart from the benefits of his concrete advice, I would not have carried this work through to completion without his support and encouragement. I also thank Joel Fried, Glenn MacDonald, Ron Wintrobe and Chris Robinson for their advice and for forcing me (sometimes unwillingly) to express my ideas with greater clarity and vigour. Roger Farmer, Peter Howitt, Michael Parkin and especially Tim Lane helped me with earlier stages in particular, and Tom Rymes and Ian Steedman read and gave detailed comments on the whole of the penultimate draft. Finally, I thank my wife, Rosslyn Emmerson, for her support, both moral and intellectual.

1

Introduction

The world which presents itself to us is partly a world composed of 'physical facts'. The fertility of the soil, the sweetness and texture of an apple, the location and size of a house, the pattern on a piece of paper, the age, height and eye colour of a fellow human being, are all examples of physical facts. A visitor from another planet, possessing the same five senses and measuring instruments as ourselves, could observe these physical facts of our world as well as we can. To a solitary being — a Robinson Crusoe — these physical facts are the only facts the world presents.

But apart from physical facts, the world also presents us with 'social facts'.[1] That this soil belongs to my neighbour, that an apple is stolen, that a house is mortgaged, that a piece of paper is money, that a woman is my wife, are all examples of social facts. A visitor newly arrived from another planet could not observe these social facts, no matter how acute his five senses or how precise his measuring instruments. Robinson Crusoe would not be aware of any such social facts.

Social facts are not reducible to physical facts. The ownership of soil is not an attribute that can be measured in the same way as its fertility. Two apples can be identical in terms of sweetness, texture, and every other physical property, yet one can be stolen and the other not. If I see an unauthorized person forging a banknote, then regardless of how perfect a copy it is of a genuine banknote, it is not money. My wife's identical twin is not my wife.

Imagine two spectators at an auction. One is newly arrived from Mars; the other is a member of our society. The first observes a sequence of body movements and utterances culminating in the banging of a hammer. The second observes a sequence of bids culminating in the purchase of a good. Though each receives exactly the same sensory impressions, what they observe is completely different. The first observes only the physical facts. The second observes the social facts.

Unless he is an anthropologist newly arrived from Papua New Guinea, the social scientist is like the second observer. He observes the social facts of bidding and exchange, and seeks to explain why people bid the amounts they do and why the price is what it is. Perhaps he may also seek to probe deeper than this, and try to explain why exchanges are sometimes conducted using this sort of open auction instead of in some other way. Only the newly-arrived anthropologist finds the social facts problematic — but his problem is not whether social facts exist, but what sort of social facts these are — is he observing an auction or some form of religious ceremony?

What I take here as problematic — as being in need of explanation — is that social facts exist at all. What sort of 'facts' are these things I have called 'social facts'? How are these facts created? How do members of society 'know' these facts and what does it mean to 'know' them?[2] Why does people's behaviour depend not only on the physical facts of their natural environment, but also on these social facts as well?[3] In short, what is society and how is it possible?

These questions are important. Of course they are important and interesting questions in their own right but, even if we were to fail to appreciate the intrinsic importance of such apparently 'philosophical' questions, we should nevertheless consider them important if only for the implications that answers to these questions might have for other, more practical questions.

The subject matter of the social sciences is largely composed of social facts. Who will buy what? Who will marry whom? Who will vote for whom to become president? These questions, the bread and butter of the social sciences, are questions about particular social facts. These questions would not even make sense to a Martian who was ignorant of the social institutions of property rights, marriage and democratic government. It is only within these social institutions that words like 'buy', 'marry', 'vote' and 'president' have any meaning. Even supposing that our Martian, observing what we know to be an auction, were able exactly to explain and predict the body movement of the participants in terms of physical laws about neurons, synapses, muscles, light waves, etc., the result would not be social science. The anthropologist would still want to know whether he was observing an auction or a religious ceremony. The economist would still want to know why the bidders bid the prices they did. Social science is largely about social facts.

It is not an unforgivable sin to practice social science while treating the very existence of the social facts you are discussing as unproblematic. It is not obvious that we shall fall into major error by seeking to explain human behaviour *within* a given framework of social institutions while treating the existence of that same social institution as an unexplained, exogenous, datum. We have to start somewhere. But it can never ultimately be satisfactory to do this. That social facts exist is itself a social phenomenon. Social institutions are, in some or other sense, man-made. The question therefore naturally arises of whether a theory that is used to explain human action and interaction within a given framework of social institutions is compatible with the existence of that social institution itself? Could the same people who participate in a social institution treated as an exogenous datum also have made that institution? If not, then that theory is placed in the very embarrassing position of being a theory which is incompatible with the existence of the social facts which are its subject matter. If that theory were true, there would be nothing for it to explain. To put it another way, the very existence of society serves as an additional test of any theory of human action within society.

The question this book addresses is then that of the nature and existence of social facts, social institutions, or society. I am not here concerned with the secondary question of which *types* of social institution will exist under which circumstances, but with the primary question of how *any* social institution can exist, and what it means to state that a social institution exists. I approach this question as an economist. Is it possible to explain the nature and existence of social institutions from the assumption of rational and self-seeking individual behaviour? In particular, could 'Homo Economicus' have created the world of private property rights and exchange which he is so commonly assumed to inhabit?

To some social scientists, the idea that selfish[4] 'Homo Economicus' could be the creator of his social world is obviously false. Durkheim, for instance, states that '. . . it is exceedingly clear that all communal life is impossible without the existence of interests superior to those of the individual'.[5] If we accept Durkheim's opinion, then the theoretical approach adopted by economists, that of seeking to explain social phenomena as the result of rational self-seeking individual behaviour, cannot be universally valid. At best, that theoretical approach could be valid only for explaining behaviour *within* a particular institutional framework, the existence of which is treated as exogenous both by the theorist and by the agents whose behaviour he studies. Such a compromise — that the economists' approach is valid for behaviour *within* an institutional framework, but invalid for behaviour *towards* that institutional framework — is inherently unsatisfactory. There is nothing internal to the theoretical approach itself which limits its applicability to certain types of human behaviour. If the limits of applicability cannot be determined a priori, we would always be uncertain as to whether a particular application was valid or invalid — whether the behaviour we seek to explain is behaviour within or towards the framework of social institutions. We would feel compelled to reject the partially valid theory in favour of a universally valid theory, which would perhaps subsume the rejected theory as a special case approximately valid within limits that are themselves specified by the more general theory.

Traditionally, the theory of rational behaviour has focused on the isolated *action* as the unit of rationality. Each action in turn can be examined in terms of whether or not it maximizes the agent's expected utility. This theoretical approach I call 'act-individualism'. I argue that act-individualism cannot explain the existence of social institutions. If act-individualism were true, then social facts, social institutions, society, could not exist. I therefore reject act-individualism in favour of 'rule-individualism' — that rationality pertains not to *actions*, but to *rules of action* rather than to actions in themselves. A rule of action is rational if, by following that rule, an agent maximizes his expected utility. An action is rational only in so far as it is part of a rational rule of action — it is neither rational nor irrational in itself.

This distinction between act-individualism and rule-individualism, as opposing *positive* theories of how people actually behave, is exactly analogous to the distinction between act-utilitarianism and rule-utilitarianism as opposing *normative* or ethical theories of how people ought to behave. Just as rule-utilitarianism requires that people ought to act in accordance with those rules which, if followed, would maximize the sum of agents' expected utilities, so rule-individualism requires that people will rationally act in accordance with those rules which, if followed, would maximize the expected utility of the follower.

The central thesis of this book is that what we call social institutions are in fact nothing more than agents rationally following rules of action, and being believed by other agents to do so.[6] When we observe interaction between rational rule-following agents we will see them behaving in ways which look anomalous from an act-individualism perspective. For instance, agents will generally refrain from stealing goods, even when it would seem much easier to steal than to buy or make those goods for themselves. It would seem very strange to a Martian, or a visiting anthropologist, that an agent should walk any distance to pick apples from (his own) tree instead of picking the physically identical apples from a nearer tree (belonging to his neighbour). The Martian or anthropologist will cope with this anomaly by proposing some sort of taboo or imaginary constraint which prevents the agent from picking apples from the nearer tree. A system of such taboos or imaginary constraints is called a social institution. But then a social institution becomes nothing more than a theoretical construction which protects the act-individualistic theory from being falsified by such anomalous behaviour. By positing such 'institutional or social constraints' in addition to the physical constraints of the natural environment, the theorist is able to make more or less accurate predictions about agents' behaviour while retaining his act-individualistic approach to rationality.

Such imaginary institutional constraints or taboos are, however, just that. It is the following of rules which in fact explains why, for instance, an agent does not pick the fruit from his neighbour's tree. He does not steal his neighbour's apples because he expects that his neighbour would punish him if he did. The reason his neighbour would punish him is not that the act of punishing is itself rational, but because it is rational for the neighbour to follow a rule of punishing, for by doing so he will deter the theft of his apples. If agents did not follow such rules, and expect other agents to follow such rules, each would pick apples indiscriminately. There would then be no social institution of property rights, no social facts of ownership, and no society.

The broad outline of the book is as follows. In Chapter 2, I pose the questions to be addressed: What is society, and how is society possible? The answer given is that what we call 'society' is identical to agents following rules, and that it is rational for an agent to follow a rule because by doing so he can influence other agents' expectations of his own future actions, and thus influence their actions to his advantage. I contrast this theory with other theories of human behaviour and of society.

The approach to the study of social institutions put forward in Chapter 2 rests on a conceptual distinction between act-individualism and rule-individualism — between discretionary action and following a rule. This distinction is developed more fully in Chapter 3. An agent who follows a rule acts as if he had precommitted his own future actions. By rejecting discretion and committing himself to a rule, the agent sacrifices his freedom to act rationally, given other agents' expectations of his actions, in order to gain the ability to influence those same expectations. Yet the only reason an agent can have for subsequently sticking to his rule in any instance, for carrying out his promise, is to maintain his reputation for doing so in future. For an agent to be able to develop a reputation requires that others base their expectations of his future actions on his past actions. If it were possible to predict the future actions of agents a priori, then knowledge of past actions would not be needed, and so reputations would be impossible, and so rule following could not be rational. But in choosing to follow a rule, agents *ipso facto* falsify the premise that their actions can be predicted a priori, thus creating the possibility for reputation. An important implication of this is that, if society is nothing other than agents following rules, then it is impossible in principle to predict social interaction a priori. Any deterministic theory of society is logically invalid.

Chapter 2 provides support for the proposed theory of social institutions by criticizing alternative theories. Chapter 4 buttresses the argument by showing how one particular example of a social institution — a system of private property rights — can exist as a result of agents' rational rule-following behaviour. Starting from an initial position resembling the Hobbesian State of Nature, a world of completely asocial agents, we show how it would be rational for agents in such a situation to choose to follow certain rules of action and that, if they did so, the outcome would resemble a world of private property rights. Of particular importance in this chapter is the analysis of the methodological role played by constructs like the Hobbesian State of Nature. The State of Nature is not intended to resemble some state of affairs which actually once existed, and from which social institutions emerged at some point in historical time. We are not conducting an equilibrium experiment but a stability experiment when we posit the State of Nature. What we seek to show is that the asocial State of Nature is, given our theory of agents' behaviour, a *disequilibrium* state of affairs, and that the true equilibrium is one in which social institutions exist. The only point of positing the asocial State of Nature is to show the force which prevents its realization, and which therefore maintains the existence of society. That force is shown to be the desire by agents to follow rules of action. When agents do not follow rules, as under act-individualism, the equilibrium is the asocial State of Nature. When they do follow rules, the equilibrium is one in which social institutions can legitimately be said to exist. Social institutions are therefore identical to agents' rule-following behaviour.

The social equilibrium that results in Chapter 4 is efficient. Given the technology and resources available to agents, no other allocation of resources could make all agents better off. Agents' rational rule-following enables them to enforce an ideal 'social contract'. An opposing theory of social institutions is Functionalism, the theory that those institutions which exist are those which are most efficient given the circumstances. In Chapter 2, I criticize the logical adequacy of Functionalism as an explanation of the existence of social institutions: the fact that *all* agents would gain if *all* agents were to respect certain institutional constraints does not entail that *each* agent would gain if *he* were to respect those constraints. Functionalism violates the tenets of methodological individualism. However, even if the efficiency of institutions does not by itself constitute an explanation of their existence, it may nevertheless be true that existing institutions are in fact efficient. The efficient institutions that are predicted to arise in Chapter 4 are a case in point. This result, however, is not general. Under other circumstances the institutions that arise as a result of rational rule-following behaviour by individual agents will not be efficient in any non-vacuous sense. Chapter 5 demonstrates that this is so, and thus completes our critique of Functionalism. The underlying reason why rational agents cannot always achieve the efficient outcome that Functionalism predicts is that agents' reputations may not always be sufficiently valuable to motivate them to stick to the rules of action that could enforce mutually beneficial exchanges. Society is imperfect because trust is imperfect.

In presenting a theory which explains social order we must be careful not to predict too much order. Even though there does generally exist a massive background of consensus without which there could be no social facts, social institutions, or society, consensus is not omnipresent. Conflict also exists, and any reasonable theory of society must allow for its existence. Chapter 6 shows that the theory of rule-following behaviour, which explains social order, can also explain the disorder which we call conflict.

In order to maintain his rights — in order to enforce his definition of the social facts — an agent must follow a rule of punishing those he perceives to be violating those rights. Whenever differences in information between agents cause two or more agents to disagree as to who has the right to do what, each, in exercising what he perceives as his rights, will be perceived by the other as violating the other's rights. Each must therefore punish this perceived violation, and these episodes of mutual punishment appear to us as conflicts, such as wars or strikes. What agents are in effect doing in such conflicts is destroying the very things of which the ownership is in dispute, thus reconstituting the consensus over what remains. Rather than being simply the opposite of consensus therefore, conflict can be seen as a side effect of the very forces which make any consensus possible.

Those who see social institutions as being created by the state, in making and enforcing laws, will find one aspect of this book very puzzling: it makes almost no mention of the state. The social equilibrium in Chapter 4, for instance, is wholly anarchic, with each individual agent creating and enforcing his own property rights. There is nothing akin to a centralized government or sovereign which defines and enforces rights.

This neglect of the role of the state could be defended on empirical grounds. There are many instances of social life governed by unwritten laws and customs where the state plays little or no role, but this is not the defence used here. The theory that the state is the creator of society is not empirically false but logical nonsense. The state is not something separate from society but cannot logically exist without it, though society can logically and does empirically exist without the state. What we call the state is just one more social institution, and we cannot assume its existence if what we seek to explain is the very existence of social institutions. The state is not a player in the game — it is an aspect of the game's equilibrium. The fact that people commonly delegate the right to enforce their rights to rightfully appointed representatives does not obviate the need for an explanation of rights. Introducing the state as an enforcer of rights does not answer the question, it merely complicates it. An appropriate initial strategy is therefore to ignore the existence of the state. Anarchy is an appropriate methodological assumption.

What is seen to be the central message of this book will depend on the audience. Those who are already committed to the view that social phenomena must be understood as the outcome of rational individual behaviour will see its central message as arguing that we must modify our theory of rational behaviour to focus on the rationality of rules of action if we wish to understand society fully. Those who are committed to some other theory of social phenomena will see its central message as arguing that the theory of rational individual behaviour, suitably modified, has a strong claim to being considered a complete social theory, able to address the central questions of social theory such as the problem of order and the existence of consensus and conflict.

Notes

1. The reader should beware that my conception of 'social facts' differs from, for example, Durkheim's. According to my usage, a fact is a 'social fact' if, and only if, it can only be *understood* if one understands the relevant social institution. Population density, for example, though it is generally in some sense 'socially determined', is a 'physical' and not a 'social fact' in my terminology, since it can be *observed* (if not perhaps *explained*) by someone ignorant of human society.

2. This way of posing my question is similar to that of Berger and Luckmann (1966). Their concept of 'habituation' seems to play a similar role in their approach as the concept of 'following a rule' does in mine, though I find 'habituation' an inadequate basis for social theory. The fact that a pattern of behaviour is repetitive, and hence predictable, does not make it in any sense social.

3. David Hume illustrates the problematic nature of social facts in a delightful passage where he compares people's respect of property rights with their respect of superstitions:

> Those who ridicule vulgar superstitions and expose the folly of particular regards to meals, days, places, postures, apparel, have an easy task, while they consider all the qualities and relations of the objects and discover no adequate cause for that affection or antipathy, veneration or horror, which have so mighty an influence over a considerable part of mankind. A Syrian would have starved rather than taste pigeon; an Egyptian would not have approached bacon. But if these species of food be examined by the senses of sight, smell, or taste, or scrutinized by the sciences of chemistry, medicine, or physics, no difference is ever found between them and any other species, nor can that precise circumstance be pitched on which may afford a just foundation for the religious passion. A fowl on Thursday is lawful food; on Friday abominable; eggs in this house and in this diocese are permitted during Lent; a hundred paces farther, to eat them is a damnable sin. This earth or building yesterday was profane; today, by the muttering of certain words, it has become holy and sacred. . . .
>
> It may appear to a careless view, or rather a too abstracted reflection, that there enters a like superstition into all the sentiments of justice; and that if a man expose its object or what we call 'property' to the same scrutiny of sense and science, he will not, by the most accurate enquiry, find any foundation for the difference made by moral sentiment. I may lawfully nourish myself from this tree; but the fruit of another of the same species, ten paces off, it is criminal for me to touch. Had I worn this apparel an hour ago, I had merited the severist punishment; but a man, by pronouncing a few magical syllables, has now rendered it fit for my use and service. . . . The same species of reasoning, it may be thought, which so successfully exposes superstition, is also applicable to justice; nor is it possible, in the one case more than in the other, to point out in the object that precise quality or circumstance which is the foundation of the sentiment.

Hume goes on to point out an important difference — that while superstition is useless, justice is useful to the functioning of society.

Such useful functions of social institutions do not, however, explain their existence.

4. I show in Chapter 7 that it does not matter whether people are *perfectly* selfish or not. The important distinction is between whether people are perfectly altruistic (in the sense of being equally concerned for another as for themselves) or only imperfectly altruistic (and caring more about themselves). Assuming that people are perfectly selfish is, however, simpler, and would seem to present me with the stronger challenge of explaining social institutions even under this extreme (and unrealistic) case.

5. The full quotation reads:

   In order to prosecute individualism more easily, (its enemies) confuse it with the strict utilitarianism and utilitarian egoism of Spencer and the economists. But that is to make the contest too easy. It is indeed an easy game to denounce as an ideal without grandeur this crass commercialism which reduces society to nothing more than a vast apparatus of production and exchange. For it is exceedingly clear that all communal life is impossible without the existence of interests superior to those of the individual. We quite agree that nothing is more deserved than that such doctrines be considered anarchical.

   (Durkheim, 1898, p. 44.)

6. Thompson and Faith (1981) have independently arrived at a theory of social institutions based on agents precommitting their actions which is close in spirit to the approach presented here. The major difference between our approaches lies in my emphasis on the need for agents' reputations in making their commitments credible.

2

Institutions are Rules of Action

2.1 The Question

The question to be addressed is this: 'from the economic perspective, how is society possible?'

The primary question of social science must be the problem of order. How is society possible? Why do we conduct our lives within a more or less shared set of social institutions such as law, language, marriage, clubs, nations, universities, markets, property rights, etc., instead of living as isolated individuals in a Hobbesian State of Nature?[1]

This primary question can, of course, be addressed from more than one theoretical approach or perspective, and the question to be addressed will change somewhat according to the theoretical approach adopted in attempting to answer it. The question is surely at its starkest when addressed from the theoretical perspective most widely adopted by (most) contemporary economists. How is it possible that social institutions of any kind could ever exist in a world populated by atomistic, self-seeking, rational individuals? Furthermore, if one accepts the methodological individualism of this economic approach and thus eschews holistic concepts, it is hard to see how one could even give an account of *what* a social institution is, never mind *why* it is.

No doubt the apparent impossibility of explaining the nature and existence of social institutions from the economic or any other individualistic perspective has sufficed for many social scientists as reason to reject such perspectives. It is thus a worthwhile enterprise to study the compatibility of the economic perspective with the existence of social institutions because a discovery that they are compatible would reinstate the economic perspective as a serious contender for being a *general* theory of social science.

What I refer to as 'the economic perspective' (or approach) is only secondarily a set of theories about narrowly-defined 'economic' phenomena, such as prices and quantities of goods traded in markets. Primarily it is an approach to the study of human action and interaction which takes as its central axiom that individuals act rationally — they act so as to maximize a well-defined and stable objective function, representing their personal preferences, subject to their information on the constraints facing them. Now if people act rationally in their purchases and sales of goods and services, why should they not act rationally in all other activities as well?[2]

The economic approach contains no internal restrictions of its scope which require that it be applicable only to what is normally thought of as the 'economic' sphere of human interaction. For those who have already adopted this approach our enterprise is worthwhile, because the only way to determine the limits of applicability of the economic approach is to keep trying to extend the applications of that approach until the limit is reached.

A third reason for pursuing our question is the most important. Economists generally study the human action and interaction which takes place *within* a given framework of social institutions. The most common examples are the institutions of private property rights and laws of contract. Indeed the very facts studied by economists are for the most part 'social facts,' such as the exchange of one good for another. Exchange is not a 'physical fact'. It is not the same as, nor does it even require, the physical movement of objects from one person to another.[3] The exchange of goods is a social fact because what is exchanged are agents' *rights* to behave in certain ways with respect to certain objects, and such rights only have meaning within the social institution of private property. A visitor from another planet, ignorant of human institutions, could observe the physical fact of the movement of objects, but could not logically observe the exchange of goods.

Taking the institutional framework as given, economists have reasonably satisfactory theories of how a change in the various parameters would affect agents' actions within that framework. If the institutional framework were indeed exogenous with respect to the parameters which determine agents' actions within that framework, then it would be perfectly legitimate to treat the framework as given. But the assumption of exogeneity is not prima facie compelling.

We know that social institutions do change; the elimination of slavery is one example of a limited dissolution of property rights. It also seems reasonable to suppose that social institutions, unlike the weather, are not exogenous to human actions and beliefs (they are in some sense man-made). It further seems unlikely that the parameters which determine those actions and beliefs which influence, create, or indeed constitute, the prevailing social institutions are totally separate from the set of parameters which determine agents' actions within that institutional framework.

There exists the possibility, therefore, that an increase in demand for a good may result, not in an increase in price and quantity exchanged, but in the disappearance of the institution of private property in that good which alone makes price and quantity exchanged meaningful concepts — an erasure of the social facts presupposed by the axes of our demand and supply diagram. Furthermore, if social institutions *are* endogenous with respect to human action then rational agents may realize that this is so. Agents would then choose their actions taking into account not only the effect of their actions within the institutional framework, but also the effect of their actions on the institutional framework itself, contrary to what is supposed when that framework is taken as given. Everyday examples of these two implications of institutional endogeneity might be where an increase in demand results in an industry being nationalized, or where a monopolist sets price below what would otherwise be a profit maximizing price for fear that a higher price might result in expropriation.

The above is not intended as a criticism of economists. It is surely a sensible procedure to ignore some problems in order to concentrate on solving others. Nor is it obvious that the assumption of institutional exogeneity has frequently led to major empirical errors, though I shall argue in Chapters 5 and 6 that some particularly problematic phenomena, such as unemployment and strikes, can be better understood by dropping the assumption of institutional exogeneity. Instead, the above is intended to motivate us to address the question of the nature and existence of social institutions from the economic perspective, by showing the potential practical importance of an answer.

2.2 Functionalism

It might be claimed that there already exists an (at least tentative) economic theory to explain the existence of (at least some) social institutions. I will cite two examples from the existing literature.

Demsetz (1967, p. 350) for example has argued that '. . . property rights develop to internalize externalities when the gains of internalization become larger than the costs of internalization.' Although the economic analysis of the costs of internalization is not well developed, we seem here to have a theory capable in principle of explaining when the institution of property rights will most likely exist.

Another example is Skogh and Stuart (1982), who analyse how a system of collectively enforced property rights can increase welfare by reducing the costs of conflict over the distribution of resources. (I draw on their analysis in Chapter 4.) They argue that property rights will emerge whenever the costs of enforcement are less than these gains.

These two papers differ in one important respect. Whereas Skogh and Stuart initially pose a world resembling the Hobbesian State of Nature which contains *no* social institution, Demsetz initially postulates a world of *common* property rights and presumes the institution of contract in his discussion of how agents would agree to convert common into *private* (excludable) property rights. Demsetz thus presents a theory of *change* in social institutions, while Skogh and Stuart present a theory of the *existence* of a social institution.

Despite this important difference the two papers have something even more important in common: their adherence to *Functional-*

ism. Prevalent in sociology and anthropology, Functionalism is an approach to the study of social institutions in terms of their functions — the needs or purposes satisfied by those institutions. Nearly all existing economic analysis of social institutions is a special variety of Functionalist analysis, which uses Pareto Optimality (efficiency) as its relevant functional criterion. (To say that a state of affairs is 'Pareto Optimal' means that it is not possible to make one person better off without making some other person worse off.)

Now there is nothing wrong or uninteresting in asking the Functionalist *question* — asking which type of social institution (including none at all) would lead to the most efficient allocation of resources under various conditions. The danger lies not with asking this question, but with the belief that in answering this question one *ipso facto* explains why that institution exists. A Functionalist analysis explains the *consequences* of the existence of an institution, and an explanation of those consequences is not in itself an explanation of the *causes* of the existence of that institution. This 'problem of illegitimate teleology' is no stranger to modern sociologists nor to the founders of the Functionalist approach in sociology.[4] A Functionalist analysis *might* provide part of an explanation for the existence of an institution, but is completed only when supplemented by an additional theory to link the consequences of an institution with the causes of its existence.

There are two natural candidates for such a link-theory. One candidate refers to the *intentions* of the agents who created the institution. Realizing that all agents would be better off under, for example, a system of private property rights (compared to any alternative institution), agents collectively agree to create just such a system. Whereas this first candidate — the 'intended-consequence' explanation — requires that social institutions be deliberately created by agents foreseeing the desirable consequences described in the Functionalist analysis, the second candidate for a theory to link consequences with causes relies on some unintended selection process.

According to the second candidate for a theory to link the consequences with the causes of an institution, less efficient (or otherwise disfunctional) social institutions will tend to lose members to more efficient competing institutions.[5] Alternatively, societies with a less efficient total set of institutions will tend to lose members to, or be destroyed in conflict with, societies with a more efficient total set. Provided this selection process operates quickly, relative to the rate of change of the underlying parameters, the social institutions observed at a point in time will be close to the most efficient set given those underlying parameters, for only the most efficient will survive in the long run.

There are problems with both these candidates for a theory to complete a Functionalist analysis linking consequences with causes.

The first candidate — the intended-consequence explanation — seems to presuppose a high degree of wisdom and foresight on the part of the founders of an institution. Moreover, if this candidate is accepted, what matters in explaining the existence of an institution is not the *actual* function of that institution, but the function which the founders of that institution *believed* it would fulfil. A Functionalist explanation of the existence of an institution would then be either an exercise in the history of ideas or else a confessedly unoriginal theory (since the founders were already aware of that theory).

The first candidate, since it maintains that institutions are chosen, also needs to specify who does the choosing. If choice were unanimous, we could be sure that only perceived Pareto Improving changes to institutions were made (some benefit, and none lose). If choices were not required to be unanimous, not all changes to institutions would be Pareto Improving. Actual institutional changes are rarely unanimous; some benefit, but others lose. The changes made depend on who has the power to effect changes. Moreover, even if actual institutions were always efficient, that efficiency might still leave the institutional structure critically indeterminate; for example, slavery and the absence of slavery may both be efficient. It might be the case that slaves could not compensate slaveowners sufficiently to make the elimination of slavery unanimous, and also that prospective slaveowners could not compensate freed slaves to make the return to slavery unanimous. Neither institutional structure is then Pareto Superior to the other.

The second candidate — that the prevailing set of institutions approaches efficiency as a result of some unintended selection process — does not require foresight and wisdom of the founders of institutions. Instead it requires a process to *generate* a wide variety of different institutions (the analogue of the biologists' spontaneous genetic mutation) and a process to *select* the more efficient of those institutions as more likely to survive than less efficient ones. It is not obvious that a suitable institution-generating process exists. It may be that the very existence of current institutions precludes the creation of potentially more efficient competitors. For example, if *all* land is initially common property how can private property rights ever begin without *ipso facto* violating common property rights? If there were a mechanism whereby those with rights to common property could renounce their rights (and those of their heirs) in return for compensation then the enclosure of commons need not violate the rights of commoners, but this mechanism would itself be part of the prevailing social institutions, and may or may not exist. Furthermore, it is not obvious that the ability of a society to survive depends totally or even mainly on the efficiency (Pareto Optimality) of its institutions. Military dictatorships might be miserable societies, but might well succeed in conflict with more hedonistic societies.

When we ask whether corporations, partnerships, customer-owned co-operatives or worker-controlled syndicates are more likely to exist in a given industry, it is reasonable to assume that it will be the more efficient form. The most efficient organization will be able to give a better deal to all interested parties and they will choose it over less efficient organizations. Except for the speed of adjustment, it does not matter whether agents realize that, for example, the corporation is the most efficient type of organization and choose it immediately, or whether corporations come to be prevalent as a result of a process of trial, error, and the mimicry of the successful.

This sort of reasoning is more or less valid *within* a given institutional framework of competition, well-defined and enforced alienable private property rights, and freedom of contract — the normal habitat of the economist. The fallacy of the economist's version of Functionalism lies in applying this same sort of reasoning in contexts *outside* that particular institutional framework and, in particular, in applying that same sort of reasoning to explain the very existence of that particular institutional framework. Corporations are unlikely to exist, for instance, in an industry where workers are able to expropriate capital at gunpoint. Freedom of contract may not be allowed to survive if it is against the interests of people with the power to curtail it. The Lord of the Manor will not pay commoners to give up their rights if they continue to graze their cattle on the common land, regardless of their right to do so.

Quite apart from the above criticisms, there is a far more fundamental inadequacy with Functionalism as a radical explanation of the emergence of social institutions *ex nihilo*. This is that it simply fails to provide an account, compatible with the methodological individualism of economists, of the *nature* of social institutions. Of what sort of stuff are social institutions made?

The economists' version of Functionalism views an institution as being a set of constraints on the behaviour of individual agents.[6] These 'institutional constraints' are modelled in exactly the same way as the constraints, for instance, on physical resources. Functionalist analysis consists of comparing the results of agents' interactions subject to different sets of these institutional constraints (the Hobbesian State of Nature having been modelled as having no such constraints at all), in terms of various desiderata such as efficiency. Now there is nothing wrong with performing this sort of exercise, nor are the answers gleaned thereby uninteresting, but it does not constitute an explanation of the existence of those constraints.

If social institutions were like physical barriers (private property rights, for instance, being an unclimbable fence around each agent's goods) then we could understand very easily why agents' behaviour would have to conform to institutional constraints. We could then easily supplement a Functional analysis to turn it into a genuine explanation of the existence of institutions. For example, we could imagine an initial stage in the game wherein agents decide whether to build such fences, and where to build them, their decisions being based on their expectations of the effects of those decisions on the outcomes in future stages of the game. This way of modelling institutional choice would correspond to the intended-consequence explanation as a candidate to link the consequences of an institution with its causes. It is not immediately obvious that agents would always choose to build the most efficient set of fences, but presumably efficiency would be *somehow* related to their choices.

Alternatively we could adopt the unintended selection process candidate for a theory to link the consequences of an institution with its causes. We would then model agents as building various types of fence more or less at random, with agents building the 'wrong' sort of fence getting lower payoffs, and either dying or else deciding to copy those building the 'right' sort of fence and getting higher payoffs. Again it is not immediately obvious that this process would always eventually converge upon a long run equilibrium with an efficient set of fences, but this *might* happen.

Social institutions, however, are not like fences. Both are man-made, but the analogy stops there. Once a fence has been constructed it has a physical existence which does not logically depend on the actions and beliefs of agents. It will not go away if we simply all stop believing in its existence. Our physical behaviour cannot be the same as if it did not exist. If we wish its non-existence we must take physical action with hammers and saws to *cause* its non-existence. None of this is true for social institutions. If every member of society were simply to stop believing in the existence of property rights then, like Tinkerbell in *Peter Pan*, they *would* no longer exist for that society. Every member can physically behave as if property rights did not exist, and if every member were to do so then they would not exist for that society. Such beliefs and actions do not *cause* the non-existence of property rights, they *logically entail it*. The existence of fences is only *causally* and *empirically* related to human action and belief; the existence of social institutions is *logically* related to human action and belief.

The fact that social institutions are logically identical to some or other facet of human action and belief means that a full understanding of social institutions requires an answer to the following two questions. What *sorts* of human action and belief constitute the social institution? And why do agents perform those actions and hold those beliefs which constitute the social institution? To answer the first question is to explain the *nature* of social institutions — to explain *what* they are. To answer the second question is to explain the *existence* of social institutions — to explain *why* they are.

Noting that social institutions are none other than some or other facet of human action and belief reveals the inadequacy of merely analysing agents' behaviour subject to various institutional constraints. What are these constraints? Why do agents not violate them? How and why do agents enforce them?

If we dropped the economists' methodological individualism our task of answering these questions would be much easier. We could then invoke the 'collectivity' as enforcing the constraints, doing so in order to reap the collective benefits. For the methodological individualist, however, the nature and existence of the collectivity (for example, the state) is as problematic as the nature and existence of the social institutions which it is invoked to explain. Indeed the state *is* but a social institution. To adopt a *partial equilibrium* explanation of some particular institution, while presupposing the existence of other institutions, is illegitimate if we seek to examine the compatibility of social institutions with the economic approach to the study of human action. For that we need a *general equilibrium*, or radical analysis, presupposing the existence of no social institution.

In sum, we need to explain the nature and existence of social institutions as some aspect of the outcome of a game between self-seeking rational individuals. We must avoid the fallacy of composition which may ensnare those who start from a Functionalist analysis. That *all* would gain if *all* were to conform to the constraints of some social institution does not entail that *each* would gain if *he* were to do so. Neither must we introduce collective entities, when seeking a radical and individualistic explanation, as *dei ex machina* to rescue individuals from their predicament in the Hobbesian State of Nature. From the economic perspective adopted here, if rational self-seeking individuals cannot escape the State of Nature by their own efforts, then there they must remain, and we must perforce reject the economic perspective (or else claim that the world we inhabit is, in fact, the State of Nature).

2.3 An Outline of the Answer

I have argued that social institutions are *identical to* (as opposed to being a mere causal product of) some or other facet of human action and belief. A social institution is nothing more than a particular way of acting and believing for some agents who are thus said to be members of, or participants in, that social institution. What sort of actions and beliefs are these that constitute social institutions? Why do rational self-seeking individuals perform these actions and hold these beliefs? An answer to these questions is to explain the nature and existence of social institutions.

My answer is that social institutions are constituted by agents following *rules of action* and believing others to follow *rules of action*. It is rational to follow a rule of action because by doing so an agent can influence other agents' expectations of his future actions, and can thereby influence their actions to his advantage. Since it is rational to follow rules of action, agents will in fact follow rules of action, and it is therefore rational to believe that agents follow rules of action.

To understand why it is rational to follow a rule, it helps first to understand the advantages of precommitment. In any interesting dynamic game between two or more agents, one agent's utility depends both on his current and future actions and on those of others. The actions chosen by those other agents also generally depend on their expectations of his future actions. Let us suppose that the one agent could precommit his future action, and reveal that precommitment to other agents. The agent will take into account not only the direct effect of his future action on his utility in choosing the action to which he commits himself, but will also take into account the indirect effect — how his current choice of commitment influences others' expectations of his future action, which expectations affect their current actions — which in turn affect the first agent's utility. Now suppose instead that the agent does not, or cannot, precommit his future action. Instead he waits until the future action is to be performed before choosing that action. By that time the other agents have already performed their actions and, being unable to influence the past actions of other agents, the agent considers only the direct effect of his action on his utility. In general, the action chosen in this discretionary manner will differ from the action chosen if he were to precommit his action.

The theory of social institutions I am proposing rests on a theory of human action which we might call 'rule-individualism' in contrast to 'act-individualism'. Under act-individualism, the unit action is the basic unit of analysis. The concept of rationality pertains to isolated actions — an action being rational if, and only if, it maximizes the agent's expected utility. Under rule-individualism it is not the isolated action, but the *method of choosing actions* — the recurring pattern, sequence, or *rule of action* — which is the basic unit of analysis to which the concept of rationality pertains. An action can be said to be rational only in so far as it is part of a rational rule of action — is chosen by a rational method of choosing actions. That rule of action is rational which maximizes the agent's expected utility. Whereas act-individualism proposes a one-step test of rationality, the action being evaluated directly in terms of its consequences, rule-individualism proposes a two-step test of rationality, the action being evaluated in terms of the rules to which it conforms, and the rule in turn being evaluated in terms of the consequences of following that rule.[7]

An agent who rationally follows a rule acts *as if* he had precommitted his actions. Just as the agent who precommits his future actions thereby influences others' expectations of his future actions, the agent who follows a rule of action influences others' expectations of his future actions in virtue of the rule which his past actions reveal him to be following. The act-individualist is an agent who ignores the effect of his method of choosing actions on others' expectations of his future actions. The rule-individualist is an agent who takes into account the effect of his method of choosing actions on others' expectations of his future actions. Just as an agent who can precommit his future actions can gain by sacrificing his later discretion in order to gain an instrument to influence others' expectations, so the rule-individualist rationally sacrifices his very rationality of action in order to gain influence over others' expectations of his actions.

When the time comes to perform an action to which an agent has precommitted himself, it is generally irrational for him to perform that action. If he could break his commitment he would do so, for the ends he sought to achieve by making that commitment (the modification of others' expectations and actions) have already been attained. Similarly, it is generally irrational in some sense for an agent to perform an action the performance of which is required by a rational rule. If the agent could violate that rule of action, without thereby affecting others' expectations that he will follow that rule in future, then he would rationally do so. The only reason an agent can have for maintaining his rule of action is that his failing to do so might adversely affect the beliefs of others that he will maintain that rule in future. In other words, the only reason for performing an action specified by a rule is to maintain one's *reputation* for doing so.

Despite the above-noted similarities between precommitment and following a rule, there is thus one important difference. Following a rule of action is like precommitting one's future actions except that there is a limit to what one can credibly precommit. If the value to an agent of violating his rule exceeds the value to him of maintaining his reputation for following it, then he will violate that rule. Since others will expect him to violate his rule under such circumstances, this limits his ability to influence their expectations of his future actions. If an agent's promises are enforced by a reliable third party inflicting unlimited penalties on an agent who violates his promises, his ability to make credible promises is limited only by his perceived *ability* to fulfil his promise. If an agent's promises are enforced only by his valuing his reputation for keeping future promises, his ability to make credible promises is limited by the perceived value of his maintenance of that reputation.

This distinction between act-individualism and rule-individualism is important, since I claim that the existence of social institutions can be reconciled with the rational individualism of the economic perspective only if we shift our attention from the rationality of *actions* to the rationality of *rules of action* — if we reject act-individualism in favour of rule-individualism.

This claim is justified most fully in Chapter 4, where I provide a model in which act-individualism leads inexorably to the Hobbesian State of Nature, but in which agents would rationally reject act-individualism for rule-individualism, and their doing so would lead to an equilibrium of which it can legitimately be said that there exists the social institution of private property. In the remainder of this chapter I consider more general arguments that rule-individualism rather than act-individualism is required to explain social institutions, and also defend individualistic against non-individualistic analyses of social institutions.

2.4 Act- versus Rule-Individualism

A particular social institution can be defined in terms of the various rights and obligations possessed by those who participate in that institution. The institution of private property in land, for example, defines particular people as being 'owners' of various mutually exclusive parcels of land. The 'owner' of an area of land has the (more or less circumscribed) right to use that land as he wishes. He also has the right to exclude others from using that land (the presence or absence of this right to exclude others is what distinguishes private from common property). He also has the right to alienate his rights — to transfer his right to use the land to another for an indefinite, definite but temporary, or infinite period of time. If an owner transfers all his rights to another, then the other now becomes the owner.

The social institution of (monogamous) marriage, as a second example, defines two marriage partners, 'husband' and 'wife', each of whom possesses certain standard rights and obligations with respect to the other. The partners are created in a 'marriage ceremony' in which each person undertakes these obligations (grants certain rights) to the other in exchange for the other's undertaking similar obligations. Just as in all other exchanges, the obligations are undertaken conditional on the other partner making a similar undertaking. If the 'bride' for instance, fails to make her 'vows,' then the 'groom's' are null and void.

The first step in the analysis of any particular social institution is to describe the set of rights and obligations possessed by participants in that institution, including the rightful ways in which possession of rights and obligations may be acquired, modified, and lost. I have sketched just such a description above for two examples of social institutions. Ultimately, all rights and obligations are rights and obligations for people to behave physically in certain ways. If I own a fruit tree, for example, I have the right to pick and consume the fruit (provided I have not let this right exclusively to another). The *actions* constituted by a particular type of physical behaviour depend on the relevant institutional framework and institutional facts. If I did not have the right to do so, my exact same physical behaviour of picking and consuming the fruit would be an act of theft. This particular act looked at in isolation, therefore, cannot tell us whether it is an act of theft or not. This in itself is an argument against the possibility of reconciling the existence of social institutions with act-individualism, where the isolated act is the basic unit of analysis.

What is it then which determines the conditions under which my physical behaviour of picking and consuming the fruit constitutes or does not constitute an act of theft? Obviously it depends on whether I own the tree, yet whether or not I own the tree depends solely on the *past* actions of myself and others. The fact that I acquired ownership in the *past* (by a *past* act of exchange or gift, etc.) and have not *previously* acted so as to renounce my ownership, *logically entails* (under the social institution of full-fledged private property) that I own the tree now. And provided I have not *previously* let the rights to the current fruit, then I have the (exclusive) right to pick and consume the fruit, and my doing so is not an act of theft. Were the facts about the *past* different, then my performing the exact same physical behaviour would constitute an act of theft. The social institution of private property is inherently backward looking.

The social institution of marriage is also backward looking. The social fact that I am now a husband and have certain rights and obligations which attach to my institutionally defined status is logically entailed by the social facts of my having partaken in the wedding ceremony and having not obtained a divorce, both of which pertain to the past. I would claim that all social institutions similarly contain some inherently backward-looking element.

It is important to note that the relation between past actions and current rights and obligations (and hence the current actions constituted by current physical behaviour) is not a mere causal relation, but one of logical entailment. This means that social institutions are not only backward looking but are *irreducibly* backward looking. We cannot substitute statements about present and future facts for statements about past facts without loss of meaning, for past, present and future physical facts can only be *causally* (or empirically), not *logically* related. Possession of a piece of paper with ink marks on it, called 'a title deed' or 'a marriage certificate' does not *constitute* ownership or marriage, it merely indicates it. Possession of a forged title deed or marriage certificate, no matter how perfect the forgery, does not mean that the possessor is owner of an area of land or that he is married. Loss of the pieces of paper does not *mean* loss of rights, it merely means loss of some part of the *evidence* of having those rights (though this may, of course, *cause* subsequent loss of rights in a legal hearing, or *cause* violation of rights through fraud or theft). It is past facts, and past facts alone, which determine one's present rights and obligations under the institutions of private property and marriage.

I have argued that social institutions contain an inherently backward-looking perspective: the rights and obligations which attach to an individual who participates in an institution depend irreducibly upon past actions. If social institutions exist then agents must pay at least some respect to the rights and obligations thereby defined. (It would be *logical* nonsense to say that the institution of private property exists, if agents made no behavioural distinction ever between their own property and the property of others.) Thus the existence of social institutions is logically incompatible with the assumption of rational act-individualism, for one of the central tenets of the latter is that bygones are bygones. A rational act-individualist chooses whichever current action has the best (for him) consequences, and consequences happen in the present and future. The past matters only in so far as it causally affects and provides information about that present and future. The past never matters irreducibly. The past *per se* never matters for a rational act-individualist. Take two rational act-individualists with the same preferences and same beliefs about the present and future and they will act in exactly the same way, no matter whether their histories are different.

This contradiction between the forward-looking, or teleological, perspective of act-individualism and the backward-looking, or deontological, perspective of social institutions is at its most obvious when we consider the institution of promising which, if my thesis is accepted, is seen as the basis of all social institutions. If all agents were rational act-individuals, then the past action of one agent in making a promise would be totally irrelevant for their subsequent behaviour. If this were true, of course, then the social institution of promising would not logically exist.

Similarly, let us consider the following mental experiment. Imagine that by some strange accident all memories and other records of debt were destroyed. It is extremely unlikely that the economy would continue to unfold in exactly the same manner as it would have had the accident not happened — that agents make exactly the same payments (of interest and principal) as they would have otherwise. (If this were not the case it would be impossible to understand why creditors bother to keep records of debt.) Now the actions of a rational act-individualistic agent depend only on his current and future preferences, his beliefs about current and future states of the world and other agents' actions. Since he knows that those other agents' actions are determined likewise, and since, by assumption, the accident does not affect preferences or beliefs about current and future states of the world (except trivially, in that some little pieces of paper have been destroyed), neither he nor any other agent will have reason to act differently as a result of the accidental loss of records and memories of debt. Thus the assumption that all agents are act-individualists (and that this is common knowledge between all agents) leads to ludicrous conclusions about the social institution of debt.

As a final criticism of the possibility of an act-individualistic analysis of social institutions (though these are all really just different aspects of the same basic criticism), let us consider how rights and obligations could be enforced if all agents were rational act-individualists. These rights and obligations are modelled as institutional constraints on agents' behaviour in Functionalist analyses of social institutions. I have argued, however, that these institutional constraints cannot be like physical barriers to agents' behaviour, and that the nature of these constraints and the causes of their existence must be explained if we seek to explain the nature and existence of social institutions.

Why does a farmer, harvesting his own corn, not cross into his neighbour's field of equally ripe corn and harvest that too? A fence between their fields, if there is one at all, is a typically trivial physical barrier. The reason he does not do so is that he fears the consequences — he expects to be punished. But would it be rational for the neighbour to punish him? If the neighbour were an act-individualist, for whom bygones are bygones, he would no more punish the farmer for stealing his corn than he would 'punish' the farmer if freak weather conditions had destroyed his crop and doubled the farmer's crop, for in both cases the current state would be the same, the neighbour having no corn in store and the farmer a double amount. It is only the past history of how that current state was reached that differs between the two cases. Yet since the past is irrelevant in a world of act-individuals, if it is not rational for the neighbour to 'punish' the farmer in the case of freak weather conditions then neither is it rational to punish in the case of stealing. Now, if it is not rational for the neighbour to punish the farmer for stealing, the farmer will know this, and will not expect to be punished, and so will therefore always steal his neighbour's corn (as indeed his neighbour will always steal the farmer's), and so there will be no institution of private property between them, and we cannot even speak of one field's being the farmer's and another his neighbour's. Act-individualistic behaviour is incompatible with the enforcement of rights, and so is incompatible with the existence of rights.

I judge these arguments above to demonstrate that the existence of social institutions cannot be reconciled with the theory of human behaviour I have called act-individualism. The basic problem is the incompatibility between the *teleological* perspective of the latter — each action being rationally chosen *in order to* best achieve the individual's *present* and *future* goals — and the *deontological* perspective of social institutions — wherein individuals act *because of past* undertaking of obligations, and wherein rights are enforced by acts of punishment performed *because of past* transgressions.

The rule-individualistic approach I am advocating in its place is immune to the above arguments against act-individualism. The neighbour will rationally *follow a rule* of punishing transgressions of his property rights, because if the farmer learns his neighbour is following such a rule he will be deterred from transgressing the neighbour's rights. An isolated act of punishment is thus neither rational nor irrational in itself; it is rational only as an instantiation of a rule of punishing, which rule it is rational to adhere to in order to influence the potential transgressor's expectations of the consequences of his actions. I perform a promised act because of my having promised to do so in the past, and I follow a rule of acting thus in order to reap the benefits that accrue to me if I can thereby get others to believe my promises.

Whereas act-individualism contains only a teleological perspective, rule-individualism contains both a teleological and a deontological perspective. Justification for acts within a rule is deontological. Justification of the rule itself is teleological.

It is only in a game against other rational individuals that rule-individualism differs from act-individualism. In a game against blind nature, there are no expectations of others to influence by following a rule, so that the behavioural prescriptions of rational rule-individualism coincide with those of act-individualism. Or, to put it another way, rules are redundant for Robinson Crusoe.

This is as it should be. If our theory of social institutions as constituted by agents following rules implied that an isolated individual could participate in a social institution, our theory would be in deep trouble. Act-individualism, in contrast, implies that there is no fundamental difference between rational behaviour in a game against nature and rational behaviour in a game against other rational agents. This is the problem that is at the root of all the problems mentioned above with providing an account of social institutions from the perspective of rational act-individualism. The economic approach to the study of human behaviour can be reconciled with the existence of social institutions only if we shift our attention away from the rationality of actions and towards the rationality of rules of action.

2.5   Individualism versus Holism?

The preceding section argues for an account of social institutions based on rule-individualism rather than on act-individualism. Many students of social institutions reject all individualistic approaches in favour of non-individualistic or 'holistic' approaches. This is particularly true of sociologists, though not all sociologists reject methodological individualism.[8] In this section I defend individualistic against non-individualistic approaches to the study of social institutions.

It must first be pointed out that the rule-individualistic approach I am advocating is less extreme in its individualism, or 'atomism', than is act-individualism. Under act-individualism the rationality of an action is formally independent of whether the agent is playing a game against blind nature or against other rational agents. The rationality of an action depends only on its expected consequences, and it makes no formal difference whether those consequences depend on the reactions of other agents, or on the 'reactions' of blind nature. The very rationality of following a rule, on the other hand, presupposes the existence of other rational agents who can comprehend the rationality of following a rule. It is because the expectations of other agents can thereby be influenced that agents rationally follow rules. Rules are meaningless in a game against blind nature, for nature has no expectations. A rule-individualistic explanation of an agent's behaviour is therefore, of necessity, an explanation involving more than one agent.

Despite this difference between act-individualism and rule-individualism, both subscribe to the central tenet of methodological individualism that all explanations of social phenomena must be based ultimately on explanations of the behaviour of individuals. It is not sufficient, for instance, to explain the behaviour of a group or class of individuals solely by reference to their group or class interests. The methodological individualist is always alert to the possibilities for free riding. As the game of prisoner's dilemma illustrates, the fact that *all* would gain if *all* were to act in a certain way does not entail that *each* would gain if *he* were to act in that way. Indeed, if this is what is meant by the aphorism, then it is not the individualist, but rather the holist who ignores the fact that the whole is not always the sum of the parts. Only if the interests of individuals were always coincident with the interests of the group would an explanation in terms of group interests suffice, for then individualistic and holistic explanations would coincide, there being no free rider problems by assumption.

Methodological individualists are hardly surprised at the idea that the interaction of individuals pursuing their own interests may result in an outcome intended by none. Nor are they surprised by the idea motivating general equilibrium theories of the allocation of resources — that agents' actions are mutually interdependent and hence explained as simultaneously determined. What then might the holistic critique of individualism amount to? How might holism reasonably differ from individualism?

In my view it is not helpful to define arbitrarily holism and individualism as contrasting positions and to argue for one against the other. More time is spent on arguing the definitions of the two positions than in examining the underlying question. This underlying question is: 'in what ways are the actions of individuals mutually related?' An extreme (and obviously false) individualistic position is to reply that they are not at all related. An extreme (and equally obviously false) holistic position is that all individuals must march in lock-step.

The economic approach to human action makes a sharp distinction between an individual's preferences and his constraints. Preferences describe how the individual ranks all conceivable outcomes, and constraints describe the individual's beliefs concerning which of the different outcomes are likely to result from all the various actions he might choose to perform. Preferences and constraints are thus simply another way of posing the traditional end–means dichotomy. The rational choice of action depends both on an agent's preferences and on his constraints.

The vast majority of economists' theories of human interaction within this tradition assume that the only way that one agent's actions affect another agent's actions is via the constraints — a change in one agent's action may change the relation between another agent's actions and their expected outcomes, and may thus change the action it is rational for him to choose. Depending on the equilibrium concept assumed by the theorist, agents may, or may not, recognize this channel of interdependence, and may, or may not, exploit in some or other way their ability thus to influence the actions of other agents.

This assumed exogeneity of preferences with respect to constraints, so that preferences influence, but are not influenced by, the results of human interaction, nor are influenced by anything which otherwise influences human interaction, is of paramount importance not only to the *particular* predictions of economic theories, but also to their having predictive content at all. Unless the determination of preference is tightly specified a priori, either as exogenous or as determined endogenously in a particular way, theories of action based on rational choice become largely vacuous.

This restriction of interdependence between agents to the single channel of the effect of actions on others' constraints, which generally passes unremarked by economists, will surely be found controversial by other social scientists. Not only is the restriction empirically dubious in its own right, but the central problem of order — how is society possible — becomes radically changed if we allow agents' preferences to be endogenous to the processes of social interaction. Perhaps society exists because (at least in part) agents internalize those values which are required for order to be possible. Perhaps the existence of the social institution of property rights depends on agents developing a *distaste* for stealing — by themselves or by others — and not merely because agents fear the external consequences of punishment should their stealing be discovered. Perhaps the practice of promising and promise keeping persists at least partly for the reason that agents come to have an intrinsic taste for keeping their promises, or at least for being known as agents who keep their promises, and not merely because they fear the indirect consequences of being unable to make credible promises in future.

I here set aside the possibility that agents' preferences are endogenous to social interaction. I do this not because I reject the possibility as empirically false; on the contrary, I think it very likely to be true. I reject it as methodologically inappropriate at this stage of the study of social institutions, for two reasons.

The first reason is that a primary motive for this study is to examine the possibility of providing an account of social institutions from the economic perspective. We seek therefore to find the *minimum possible* modifications to the economic perspective that need be made to provide an account of social institutions.

The second, more fundamental, reason is that tastes for keeping promises or for not stealing, etc., are quite different from tastes for, say, beer or music, even though both may be learned, and even learned as a result of being taught by others. Beer or music can exist for a Robinson Crusoe, promises and stealing cannot. We cannot explain the existence of the institution of promising by proposing broken promises as an argument in agents' utility functions. Quite apart from any problem of the vacuity of such an 'explanation' there is the question-begging circularity of such a procedure. That broken promises exist as an object over which preferences can be defined presupposes the very existence of the institution of promising, the explanation of which is the purpose of such an assumption. Stealing cannot logically exist without property rights, so to argue that property rights exist because agents dislike stealing is to reason in a circle.

That people dislike stealing *per se* may be true. It may also explain why stealing is not more common than it is. But it cannot logically explain the existence of property rights. We therefore must assume that agents are indifferent to stealing (meaning by this that they get the same utility from consuming an orange whether their doing so is an act of theft or not) if we seek validly to explain the existence of property rights. Any development of preferences over social, as opposed to physical, facts is logically posterior to the existence of the social institutions which define those social facts. The analysis of any such development of preferences over social facts, though a worthwhile exercise, is beyond the scope of this study.

Notes

1. To argue that a Hobbesian State of Nature cannot persist because the human race would soon die out if it lived thus, though perfectly correct, is quite beside the point. How is it that we continuously avoid sliding into a Hobbesian State of Nature and so becoming an evolutionary dead end?
2. This view of economics goes back at least to Robbins (1932). More recently, Gary Becker in particular has attempted to push the economic approach well beyond the traditionally perceived 'economic' sphere.
3. See for instance Angell's (1929, p. 88) description of monetary exchange on the island of Uap, where virtually immobile large stones are used as money. What is interesting about this description is *not* the peculiarity of the Uap islander's behaviour — our electronic 'transmission of funds' is no less peculiar. It is interesting because by forcing us to adopt the perspective of a visiting anthropologist, and to set aside our attitude of taking social facts for granted, it forces us to see *all* social

facts as problematic. Hume (1777) creates the same effect by comparing the social facts created by the institution of property with the social facts created by religious institutions.

4. See for example, Turner (1978, p.105) for a modern sociologist's acount of the problem. Durkheim (1895, p.90) states the problem clearly: 'But this method confuses two very different questions. To show how a fact is useful is not to explain how it originated or why it is what it is.' This does not mean, however, that Durkheim always respected the distinction.

5. Hayek seems to ascribe to this second version of Functionalism when he states: 'The reason why such rules will tend to develop is that groups which happen to have adopted rules conducive to a more effective order of actions will tend to prevail over the groups with a less effective order.' Hayek (1973, p.99). It should be noted that although Hayek, like me, emphasizes rules, his concept of a rule is that of a customary or habitual pattern of behaviour which people follow because it is too costly and difficult to calculate accurately the consequences of alternative actions. He ignores what is central to my concept of a rule — that by following a rule an agent can influence others' expectations of his future actions.

6. See, for example, Schotter (1981).

7. The distinction between act-individualism and rule-individualism is thus exactly analogous to the distinction between act-utilitarianism and rule-utilitarianism. The difference is that the latter pair are both normative theories about how people ought morally to behave, whereas I am concerned with the positive question of how they do in fact behave.

8. For a modern example of a more individualistic approach to sociology, see, for instance, Hechter (1983).

3

Rules and Reputation

In Chapter 2 I argued that social institutions are constituted by agents' following rules of action. It is possible to provide an account of social institutions in terms of rule-individualism but not in terms of act-individualism. In this chapter I examine more closely the difference between these two theories of rational behaviour, and explain why it can be rational for an agent to follow a rule of action.

3.1   The Borrowing Game

The advantages of being believed to follow a rule arise in contexts where the agent's optimal plans exhibit time-inconsistency.[1] I present some simple games to illustrate the time-inconsistency problem.

The first game we may call the Borrowing Game. Alan is hungry now, but will not get food until tomorrow. Bert has food now, but is not currently hungry, and has no method of storing food until he is hungry. Both could be better off if Bert gives his food to Alan today, and Alan gives his food to Bert tomorrow, but is this what will happen?

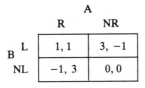

Figure 3.1

A plausible payoff matrix for the Borrowing Game is shown in Figure 3.1.

Here, L and NL represent Bert's actions of lending and not lending food. R and NR represent Alan's actions of repaying and not repaying the loan. The left number in each quadrant represents Alan's payoff, the right number represents Bert's payoff. The same game can also be presented in extensive form, revealing the order of moves, as in Figure 3.2.

Bert moves first. Bert knows that whichever move he makes, Alan will get a higher payoff by playing NR than by playing R. Bert therefore expects Alan to play NR. Bert's payoff under (NL, NR) is higher than his payoff under (L, NR) and so Bert plays NL. Each player thus gets a payoff of zero. Both would be better off under (L, R) where each gets a payoff of one.

The Borrowing Game has an identical payoff matrix to the familiar game of Prisoner's Dilemma, and the outcome is the same. The

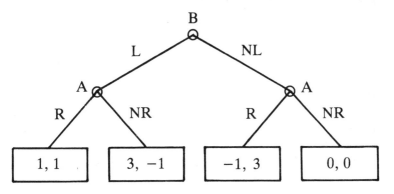

Figure 3.2

only difference is that in Prisoner's Dilemma the moves are made 'simultaneously' — each player makes his move in ignorance of the other's move — whereas in the Borrowing Game Alan makes his move knowing what move Bert has made.

Unlike Prisoner's Dilemma, the Borrowing Game is more than just a curiosity. *All* exchanges are examples of the Borrowing Game, for each agent gives up something he values in return for something he values more highly. What the Borrowing Game seems to tell us, however, is that exchange is impossible between rational agents, for the outcome of the Borrowing Game is that neither player will hand over his goods to the other.

How then is exchange possible? Given the purpose of this enquiry, it is not sufficient to reply that exchange is possible because it is enforced by law — that Alan will be punished by third parties if he accepts Bert's loan, but does not repay it. To accept this reply would be to explain one social institution, exchange, by assuming the existence of another social institution, law. If we wish to examine the compatibility of the existence of social institutions with the assumption of rational individual behaviour we may not adopt such a question-begging procedure. To put this same point somewhat differently, we cannot assume, but would have to demonstrate, that those third parties would indeed rationally punish Alan for failing to repay the loan, and that it is rational for Alan to expect them to do so.

3.2   The Punishing Game

Consider now a game we may call the Punishing Game. Andrew cannot physically prevent Bill from stealing and consuming Andrew's food. Andrew can however punish Bill after the fact, but it is costly for Andrew to do so. Let S and NS stand for Bill's actions of stealing and not stealing, and P and NP stand for Andrew's actions of punishing and not punishing.

Bill knows that, whether he chooses S or NS, Andrew's payoff under NP is greater than under P, and so Andrew will choose NP. Bill's payoff under (S, NP) exceeds that under (NS, NP), and so he will choose S. Thus Bill will steal and Andrew will not punish him. See Figure 3.3.

Notice that the assumption that it is costly for Andrew to punish

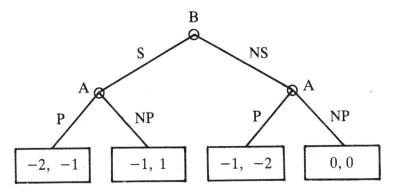

Figure 3.3

Bill is not necessary for our conclusion that Bill will steal. If instead we assumed that punishing Bill yielded benefits to Andrew, then Andrew would now punish Bill, but Bill would expect to be punished whether or not he steals, and so would still choose to steal. Only if it were both costly for Andrew to punish Bill if Bill does not steal, and beneficial to Andrew to punish Bill if Bill does steal, would Andrew punish Bill if, and only if, Bill steals. Only in this circumstance might Bill choose not to steal, for the benefits of stealing might then be less than the costs of being punished that stealing would trigger. Something similar is also true of the Borrowing Game. One would have to assume that Alan enjoys giving food when he has received food, and dislikes giving food otherwise, in order to create an incentive for Bert to give food to Alan.

If the payoff matrices of the Borrowing Game and of the Punishing Game seem plausible, then it is hard to see how the practices of exchange and of respect for property rights — surely the two most important economic institutions — could ever occur. Something must therefore be wrong with our analysis of these practices.

Suppose that the player who moves second, whom we shall call 'A' (referring either to Alan or Andrew) could *precommit* his future moves before the other player, 'B', makes his move, and reveal this precommitment to B. Given this option, A would rationally choose to precommit his future action contingent on B's action. Alan would precommit himself to giving food to Bert if and only if Bert gives food to Alan. Andrew would precommit himself to punish Bill if and only if Bill steals. Faced with such precommitments, Bert would give Alan food and Bill would not steal from Andrew.

By thus precommitting his future action, A can influence B's action to A's advantage. When the time comes to carry out his precommitment, however, A may have an incentive to break that commitment. If Bert believes Alan's precommitment, and therefore gives food to Alan, Alan could gain by not repaying the loan, which would mean breaking his commitment, and if Bert anticipated that Alan would do this, he would never make the loan in the first place. The case is slightly different in the Punishing Game. There, if Bill believes Andrew's precommitment Bill will not steal, and Andrew's incentive is not to punish, which accords with his commitment. It is if Bill does *not* believe Andrew's commitment, and does steal, that Andrew's incentive not to punish Bill would lead Andrew to break his commitment, and if Bill anticipated that Andrew would do this, then he would in fact steal.

In the Borrowing Game, Alan's precommitment has the nature of a *promise* to Bert. Bert wants Alan to make the precommitment and wants to be able to trust him to keep his precommitment. In the Punishing Game, Andrew's precommitment has the nature of a *threat*. Bill does *not* want Andrew to precommit, and does *not* want that precommitment to be credible.

Despite these differences in the two games, they share one important feature with many other dynamic games — the time-inconsistency of optimal plans. The plan of action to which A would optimally reveal himself to be committed (which may be a plan of action contingent on B's moves or on the state of the world) is such that, under at least some circumstances, A would have an incentive to depart from that plan at the later date when those actions are to be performed.

The following game reveals the most basic form of the time-inconsistency problem, and illustrates the generality of the problem.[2]

Both players choose from a wide continuous range of possible actions. Let x designate A's choice of action, performed in period two, and let y designate B's choice of action, performed in period one. A's utility is a function of both x and y:

$$U_A = U(y,x) \tag{3.1}$$

B's utility function is suppressed for simplicity, and B is assumed to have a simple reaction function wherein B's choice depends on the action B expects A to perform, x^e:

$$y = y(x^e) \tag{3.2}$$

We assume that everything in the game is common knowledge between A and B.

Suppose A can precommit his future action and reveal this precommitment to B before B moves. If B believes A's precommitment x, then $x^e = x$. To find A's optimal action under precommitment substitute B's reaction function into A's utility function and A's choice problem becomes:

$$\underset{x}{\text{Max }} U_A = U(x,y(x)) \tag{3.3}$$

Assuming an interior solution, A's optimal choice is such that:

$$\frac{\delta U}{\delta x} + \frac{\delta U}{\delta y} \cdot \frac{\delta y}{\delta x} = 0 \tag{3.4}$$

Solving equations 3.2 and 3.4 simultaneously yields an (assumed to be unique) equilibrium pair of actions $\{x^p, y^p\}$, the precommitment outcome.

Suppose now that A reconsiders his precommitment in period two. Since B's action is now predetermined, it is parametric to A's choice, and maximizing equation 3.1 with respect to x yields:

$$\frac{\delta U}{\delta x} = 0 \tag{3.5}$$

Notice the difference between equations 3.4 and 3.5. In 3.4, A takes into account not only the *direct* effect of his choice on his utility (the first term) but also the *indirect* effect (the second term) whereby his choice affects B's expectation, which affects B's action, which in turn affects A's utility. Only if B's action did not depend on his expectation of A's action ($\delta y/\delta x = 0$), or if B's action did not affect A's utility ($\delta U/\delta y = 0$), would the second term in equation 3.4 be zero and 3.4 and 3.5 would coincide. Only in special cases will one of these conditions hold, so that in general A's choice differs depending on whether it is derived from equation 3.4 or equation 3.5.

If A cannot precommit, and B knows this, then B knows that A will use equation 3.5. This 'discretionary' equilibrium $\{x^d, y^d\}$ is found by solving equations 3.2 and 3.5 simultaneously. A third possible outcome, where B is fooled into thinking that A will keep his optimal commitment, x^p, and so chooses y^p, but where A subsequently breaks his commitment, is found by substituting $y = y^p$ into 3.5 and solving for $\{x^c, y^p\}$, the 'cheating' equilibrium.

This discretionary equilibrium is simply the Nash equilibrium — each takes the other's action as given. The precommitment equilibrium is the Stackelberg equilibrium[3] — A picks his optimal point on B's reaction function. The cheating equilibrium (if it deserves the title of an 'equilibrium') is where B expects the Stackelberg equilibrium and then A actually plays Nash to B's action.

The three equilibria can be ranked unambiguously in terms of the level of utility they yield to A. The cheating equilibrium is as good or better than the precommitment equilibrium, since A can always choose an action which coincides with his commitment if he wishes to, and the precommitment equilibrium is as good or better than the discretionary equilibrium, since A can always choose to commit himself to that action which he would choose under discretion. Unless by chance all three equilibria coincide, the preference ranking is strict — each being *strictly* better than the next ranked.

Under precommitment, A imposes a constraint on his future actions. Paradoxically, this constraint increases A's utility because it enables him, in effect, to *choose* B's expectation of A's future action, though subjecting A to the constraint of having subsequently to validate B's expectation. Ideally, A would like to have it both ways, to be able both to choose B's expectation by getting B to think that A is constrained to play x^p, and actually to remain unconstrained, as occurs in the cheating equilibrium. The worst case for A occurs if A actually does commit himself to x^p, but B does not believe this commitment and, expecting x^d, plays y^d. Here A suffers the disadvantages of the constraint without thereby influencing B's expectation. (A fifth possibility is where A can get B to believe that A is committed to perform *any* action whatsoever, not merely to an action which it would be rational for A actually to commit himself. But then B would never rationally believe such a commitment, for he would know that A would only make it if he intended to break it.)

We have seen that the outcome of the game depends on two things: firstly it depends on whether A uses equation 3.4 or equation 3.5 to choose his action; secondly it depends on whether B *expects* A to use equation 3.4 or equation 3.5 to choose his action. These four combinations give rise to the four possible equilibria. Which of these four possible equilibria is *the* equilibrium? Which method of choosing actions is it *rational* for A to adopt? If we knew which method it would be rational for A to adopt, then B could know this too, and we would then know what method it would be *rational* for B to *expect* to adopt.

If B expects A to adopt the method of equation 3.4 then B will play y^p. It is then rational for A to adopt the method of equation 3.5 and play x^c, for A prefers the cheating equilibrium to the precommitment equilibrium. If B expects A to adopt the method of equation 3.5 then B will play y^d. It is then rational for A again to adopt the method of equation 3.5 and play x^d, for A prefers the discretionary equilibrium to the 'worst' equilibrium $\{x^p, y^d\}$. In both cases B's action is parametric to A's future action and it thus pays A to treat it as such, as he does in using equation 3.5. Thus regardless of the method that B expects A to use, if that expected method is independent of the method A actually adopts, then it is rational for A to adopt the method of equation 3.5.

Only if the expected method is not independent of the method actually adopted can it be rational for A to adopt the method of equation 3.4. Suppose that by choosing the method of equation 3.4 instead of 3.5, A gets B to expect the method of equation 3.4 instead of 3.5. A can thus choose the precommitment equilibrium by adopting equation 3.4, or the discretionary equilibrium by adopting equation 3.5. A, by preferring the former to the latter, would then rationally adopt the method of equation 3.4.

In the single, never to be repeated, game, with no external mechanism for making conspicuous precommitments, there is no way for A to communicate to B which of the two methods he chooses to adopt. B's expectation of A's method is therefore independent of the method actually adopted by A. It is therefore rational for A to adopt the 'discretionary' method of equation 3.5. B knows that this is so, and therefore expects A to adopt the discretionary method. The outcome is therefore the discretionary equilibrium $\{x^d, y^d\}$. In the Borrowing Game no exchange occurs. In the Punishing Game, B steals and is not punished, so property rights are not respected.

These valid conclusions — no exchange, no property rights — are obviously descriptively false. How might we modify our assumptions so as to reverse these conclusions?

3.3   Repeated Games

How might we modify our assumptions to allow exchange and respect of property rights to be possible?

One way to do this is to postulate a taste for rendering a quid pro quo, for revenge, or for respect for others' rights. This amounts to changing the payoff matrices of the games. I argued in Chapter 2 that we must reject this course if we wish to avoid a vacuous and circular explanation of social institutions.

Another way to do this is to introduce a third party into our analysis to enforce the commitments made by A. This course would be valid if we sought only a *partial equilibrium* analysis of institutions — assuming the existence of the law of contract, of judges and police in order to explain other institutions — but we seek a *general equilibrium* analysis — we seek to explain society solely on the basis of rational individual behaviour. The behaviour of those third parties cannot be assumed, but must in itself be explained in accordance with rational individualism. The possibility for enforcement of commitments by third parties would itself be a Punishing Game, so it merely postpones the problem and does not solve it.

A third way to modify our assumptions, a modification we shall explore in depth, is to suppose that instead of a single game we have a repeated game. Suppose it is known that A will repeat the same game in future, either with this same or other partners B, and that subsequent partners can observe A's history of play in similar past games. Might not then A be able to develop a *reputation* for adopting one or other method?

Suppose that A had followed the precommitment method of equation 3.4 in the past, as revealed by repeated plays of x^p, might not then B expect A to do the same in identical future games? Suppose instead that A had followed the discretionary method of equation 3.5 in the past, as revealed by repeated plays of x^d, might not then B expect A to do the same in identical future games? If this assumption is correct, then A would indeed have an incentive to adopt the precommitment method and play x^p. By playing x^p instead of x^d in this game, A sacrifices current utility, but by preserving or creating an expectation in B that he will play x^p rather than x^d in future games, he gets B to play y^p rather than y^d in future games, which increases A's payoffs in the future. Under some (but not all) parameter values (for the payoff matrix and discount rate) the discounted future gains will exceed the current losses and A will rationally choose x^p rather than x^d. Thus A could act *as if* he had made an optimal precommitment (in some circumstances), and so if B has the same knowledge as A, then B would rationally expect A to act thus (in those same circumstances).

Is the above argument valid? Before exploring what I consider to be the central problem with its validity I wish to digress to explore a well-known problem that arises when the number of repetitions of the game is known and finite.

Suppose that it is common knowledge between A and B that the game will be played N times, where N is some finite number. When the last game comes it will be exactly like the single game. A will not care about influencing B's expectation of A's behaviour in future games, for there will be no future games, and so A will follow the discretionary method, and play x^d. B will know this and, expecting x^d, will play y^d. Now consider the penultimate game. We have already established that B will play y^d in the final game, and since A knows everything that we know, A knows this too. But if A can deduce that B will play y^d in the final game, without making any assumption about A's previous plays, it must be the case that B will play y^d in the final game regardless of A's play in the penultimate game. Therefore A will rationally play x^d in the penultimate game as well, and B will know A will do this, and will therefore play y^d in the penultimate game. We can now repeat the argument and deduce that the outcome will be the discretionary equilibrium $\{x^d, y^d\}$ in game N-2, and in N-3, and so on.

Now this 'hangman' argument has generally been held to eliminate the possibility of reputation in games with a known finite number of repetitions, but to leave open the possibility of reputation in infinitely repeated games (or in games with a non-zero probability of being repeated at all points in time). In the infinitely repeated game, or supergame, there is no final game from which the mathematical induction of the hangman argument can proceed backwards. I disagree. What drives the hangman argument is the assumption that it is possible to predict A's future moves a priori, and hence predict them independently of A's previous moves. Given this premise, a similar argument can be applied to the infinitely repeated supergame as well.

The central axiom underlying the research program of game theory is the assumption of 'decidability' — that given that the game theorist knows the basic parameters of agents' preferences and information it is possible, at least in principle, to deduce the outcome of any game, at least up to an irreducibly random element. It is not so much that the game theorist asserts the truth of the decidability axiom, rather he accepts it as a methodological command to attempt to deduce outcomes from assumptions about basic parameters. The decidability axiom is the 'positive heuristic' of game theory.[4]

Let us assume that the game we are now considering is in fact decidable. This means that we, the theorists, are able to predict a priori the outcomes of the supergame (up to an irreducibly random element to allow for the possibility of mixed strategies) from knowledge of the basic parameters. We do not need to observe the history of play in order to predict future outcomes. Now we have assumed that the basic parameters of the game are common knowledge between the players A and B. This means that if the theorist can predict the outcomes of future games a priori, as is assumed when we assume the game is decidable, then so can the players. Now the only incentive A can have for adopting the precommitment method and playing x^p is if his doing so might affect B's beliefs about how A will play in future games. Given decidability and common knowledge, however, B already knows a priori how A will play in future games, and A knows this, and so A has no incentive to play x^p. A will therefore adopt the discretionary method, B knows he will do so, and the outcome will be the discretionary equilibrium $\{x^d, y^d\}$.

Given decidability and common knowledge, therefore, reputation is impossible. Conversely, reputation is possible only if either there is not common knowledge, or else the game is not decidable. To understand this result better, notice that when we argued *for* the possibility of reputation, we assumed that B's expectation of A's future action depended on A's past actions, and that A knew this. When we argued *against* the possibility of reputation, on the other hand, by assuming decidability and common knowledge we, in effect, assumed that B's expectation of A's future action was determined by the basic parameters, and hence was independent of A's past actions and that A knew this. The possibility of reputation depends crucially on how B's expectations are formed. Both assumptions about B's expectation formation seem reasonable. On the one hand, A's previous plays seem a perfect indicator of his future plays, for past and future games are identical. On the other hand, if B already knows everything about the basic parameters which underlie A's choice, A's previous plays can give B no additional information about those basic parameters which could lead him to revise his expectations about A's future choices.

My answer to this paradox is to reject the decidability axiom. It is not possible, even in principle, for the theorist to deduce a priori, from knowledge of the basic parameters of players' preferences and information alone, how rational players will act in all games. To see what is wrong with the decidability axiom, notice that if the game is decidable, then the outcome must be the discretionary equilibrium $\{x^d, y^d\}$. If on the other hand the game is not decidable, then neither the theorist nor the player B can predict A's future plays a priori, and must instead use A's past plays as an indicator of how A is likely to play in future games. If this is so then it is possible for A to establish a reputation and the precommitment equilibrium $\{x^p, y^p\}$ becomes possible. Now A prefers the precommitment equilibrium to the discretionary equilibrium, so A would wish that the game were undecidable so that B could not predict A's plays a priori. It is very easy now for A to make this game undecidable. Given decidability the equilibrium is $\{x^d, y^d\}$, and so B will predict a priori that A will play x^d. Simply by playing x^p instead of x^d, A can falsify B's a priori prediction, and force B to form his expectations a posteriori, by observing A's past plays.

It is always an option for an agent with free will to falsify a prediction one might make about his behaviour. He might rationally do so purely in order to destroy the basis of your ability to predict his behaviour. This is exactly what A does when he plays x^p. A's playing x^p (or anything other than x^d) *logically contradicts* the assumption that the game is decidable. Faced with an undecidable game, B can only use A's past action as a guide to forecasting A's future actions, which is exactly what A intends when he plays x^p. Observing x^p, B expects A to play x^p in similar future games, and so B replies with y^p, which is also exactly as A intends.

Underlying the above argument is a fundamental problem in discovering equilibria in dynamic interactive games of this sort. In deciding whether or not a given pair of strategies is a Nash equilibrium the theorist adopts the following procedure. He conjectures that an arbitrarily chosen pair of strategies is an equilibrium, and then checks his conjecture by seeing if either agent would have an incentive to depart from his conjectured equilibrium strategy, assuming that the other player will stick to his conjectured equilibrium strategy. If the answer is negative, for both players and for all conceivable ways of departing from the conjectured equilibrium, then the conjecture is verified, and the conjectured equilibrium is in fact an equilibrium (but not necessarily the only equilibrium).

In single period games, where both players move simultaneously (for instance, in ignorance of the other's move), this procedure for establishing equilibria is unproblematic. One player's departure from equilibrium cannot affect the other player's choice because the other player makes his choice in ignorance of the first player's choice. In multiperiod games, where players make their choices knowing the moves previously made by other players, the procedure can be problematic. If A were to depart from his conjectured equilibrium strategy, his doing so might affect B's subsequent moves, for B would learn of A's departure. Whether or not it would be rational for A to depart from a conjectured equilibrium strategy (and thus whether or not that strategy is in fact an equilibrium strategy) depends on how B would react to A's departure.

Selten's (1975) concept of a 'perfect equilibrium' (later refined by Kreps and Wilson's (1982) 'sequential equilibrium') was introduced to answer this question. Selten requires that an equilibrium specify a pair of strategies which state what each player will do in all possible circumstances, whether those circumstances would occur in equilibrium or not, and that in any circumstance players will subsequently follow, and be expected to follow, strategies which are equilibrium strategies in those circumstances.

To illustrate the consequences of restricting equilibria to perfect equilibria, consider the Punishing Game described above. The pair of strategies where Bill does not steal, and Andrew punishes if, and only if, Bill steals, is a Nash equilibrium. Given Andrew's strategy, Bill does best not to steal. Given that Bill does not steal, it costs Andrew nothing to follow a strategy which 'threatens' punishment if Bill steals, for he never has to carry out that threat in equilibrium. But if Bill *were* to depart from this equilibrium, and steal, it would not be rational for Andrew to maintain his strategy and punish Bill, nor for Bill to expect him to do so. Thus this is not a *perfect* equilibrium. The only perfect equilibrium is where Bill steals and Andrew does not punish.

I accept this application of the perfect equilibrium concept to eliminate non-credible threats and promises in simple, non-repeated games. It simply requires that one player, in considering a departure from a conjected equilibrium strategy, assumes that the other player will react rationally. However, in a more complex game, where some player moves more than once, or in a repeated game, application of the perfect equilibrium concept is not so straightforward.

Whether or not it is rational for A to depart from a conjectured equilibrium strategy depends on how B would react to A's departure, but how B would rationally react may depend on B's expectations of A's future actions. How might B's expectations of A's future moves be affected by B's observing a *disequilibrium* move by A? Selten's answer is that B would expect A to make only equilibrium moves subsequently. Play will proceed in a subgame, and be expected to proceed, as if play had started at that subgame. The history of previous moves required to reach that subgame is irrelevant for future play.[5] It is as if B interprets A's previous departure from his conjectured equilibrium strategy as a 'mistake' — the result of A's 'trembling hand' — and his having observed one mistake does not lead him to believe that A will make further mistakes.

If we apply this same reasoning to our infinitely repeated supergame we see that the only equilibrium is the discretionary equilibrium — where A repeats x^d each period and B, expecting x^d, plays y^d each period.

To see that the discretionary equilibrium is a perfect equilibrium in the supergame, let us first conjecture that it is an equilibrium, then see if A has an incentive to depart from x^d. If A plays anything other than x^d, then B would interpret A's departure as a mistake, and would expect A to play the equilibrium move x^d in all future games, and so B would not change his play from y^d as a result of A's departure. Now if B reacts (or fails to react) to A's departure from x^d in this manner, then A loses by departing from x^d, for the latter, by definition, is A's rational move taking B's playing y^d as given.

To see that the precommitment equilibrium cannot be a perfect equilibrium in the supergame, we first conjecture that it is an equilibrium, and then show that A has an incentive to depart from x^p. Given our conjecture that $\{x^p, y^p\}$ is an equilibrium, B will be expecting x^p, and will reply with y^p. If A were to depart from x^p, B would interpret this as a mistake, and would continue to expect the conjectured equilibrium play of x^p in the future, and so B would not change his play from y^p as a result of A's departure. Now, if B reacts (that is, fails to react) to A's departure from x^p in this way, then A gains by departing from x^p and playing x^c. Thus the precommitment equilibrium is not a perfect equilibrium.

The only reason that A can have for playing x^p rather than x^d is if his doing so leads B to expect A to play x^p rather than x^d in future games, but according to the perfect equilibrium solution this cannot be. Reputation is possible only if B's expectation of A's future moves is correlated with A's past moves, but if B interprets A's departures from a conjectured equilibrium as 'mistakes', never to be repeated, then this implies no correlation, and entails that reputation is impossible.

Given common knowledge and the perfect equilibrium solution, reputation is impossible even in the infinitely repeated supergame. Since reputation does exist (since otherwise property rights and exchange would not exist) we must either reject the assumption of common knowledge or else reject the perfect equilibrium solution. Whereas my answer to this dilemma is to reject the perfect equilibrium solution, it is worthwhile at this point to digress to consider the alternative answer, provided by Kreps and Wilson (1982) and Milgrom and Roberts (1982) who establish the possibility of reputation by dropping the assumption of common knowledge.

Let us suppose that there are three 'types' of player A. The first type, A^1, is the 'normal' rational player as described above. The second type, A^2, is a mechanism which simply repeats x^p each period. The third type, A^3, is also a mechanism which simply repeats x^d each period. (Alternatively, we could assume that the two abnormal types are not mechanisms, but have different preferences leading them to play x^p or x^d regardless of how B plays.) Player A knows his own type, but player B does not, knowing instead that there is some probability that he is playing against each of the three possible types.

I now sketch the argument used by Kreps and Wilson, and Milgrom and Roberts to show that reputation is possible (under some parameter values) in this sort of game by A choosing to imitate the behaviour of A^2.

First conjecture that A^1s equilibrium strategy is to play x^d each period. If A plays x^p, B learns that A is of type 2, and expects x^p in future. If A plays x^d, B learns that A is of type 1 or 3, and expects x^d in future. But if B forms his expectations this way then A^1 could fool B into thinking he is A^2 by departing from his conjectured equilibrium strategy and playing x^p. For low discount rates, the value to A of $\{x^p, y^d\}$ in the first game and $\{x^p, y^p\}$ thereafter will exceed that of $\{x^d, y^d\}$ permanently, and A^1 would rationally depart from the conjectured equilibrium, so the conjecture is false.

Now instead conjecture that A's equilibrium strategy is to play x^p

each period. If A^1 were to depart from this strategy and play x^d, B would believe he is playing against A^3, and would expect x^d there-'after. For low discount rates, A^1's one period gain from doing this would be exceeded by his permanent losses, so A^1 would not rationally depart from the conjectured equilibrium, and the conjecture is thus verified.

It is thus possible for reputation to exist in a perfect (or sequential) equilibrium provided we drop the assumption of common knowledge and introduce the right sorts of extra 'abnormal' types of player. A's move in one period influences B's expectations of A's future moves (as is required for reputation to exist) because it gives B information on A's type. For several reasons, however, I do not find this solution to be satisfactory.

The first reason is that in the game above, with the two abnormal types A^2 and A^3, if A^1 were ever to lose his reputation, by playing x^d, he could *never* restore his reputation. By playing x^p for some periods, and then playing x^d, he would reveal himself to be of the first type. With A's type now common knowledge, the only subsequent perfect equilibrium is the discretionary equilibrium $\{x^d, y^d\}$, as we have already established. This seems to be empirically false. A player's cheating once does not eliminate forever the chances of his again being trusted.

A second reason for dissatisfaction is that the introduction of additional abnormal types is arbitrary, and the equilibrium which results is sensitive to which additional types are introduced. What is crucial about the additional types introduced above, for instance, is that there is a positive (indeed perfect) correlation between their moves in successive periods. This implies that if B observes $x^p(x^d)$ one period, he will expect $x^p(x^d)$ again in the future, as is required if A is to have an incentive to establish a reputation. If instead the moves of the abnormal types were *negatively* correlated between periods, then if B observes $x^p(x^d)$ one period, he will expect $x^d(x^p)$ the next, and it will *not* be possible for A to establish a reputation.

There is a third reason for dissatisfaction with this explanation of reputation. We have already argued that an 'explanation' of why people keep promises which assumes that they have a taste for doing so is vacuous and circular. We are not born with an ability to change our tastes for doing x simply by uttering the words 'I promise to do x'. (How strange that people of different languages have different tastes!) It would not be a satisfactory explanation of the institution of promising which simply assumed that *everyone* had a taste for keeping promises. An explanation which assumes that even *some* people have a taste for keeping promises (the abnormal type), and that other people would choose to mimic them, is little better.

For the three reasons above I do not choose to follow Kreps and Wilson, and Milgrom and Roberts, in rejecting common knowledge in order to obtain a perfect equilibrium with reputation. Instead, I take the other horn of the dilemma, and reject the perfect equilibrium concept.

In order to ascertain whether a pair of strategies is an equilibrium, we must first conjecture that it is an equilibrium and then examine whether either player would rationally depart from his conjectured equilibrium. In conjecturing that a pair of strategies is an equilibrium pair, we simultaneously conjecture that the players also know that it is an equilibrium pair. Now if B observes A's departure from the conjectured equilibrium strategy, and if B knows that it is a departure from the equilibrium strategy, then B is faced by a logical contradiction between his knowledge of how A will *rationally* move and how A has *actually* moved. How will B react in the face of such a contradiction? We *must* answer this question, because whether A's strategy *is* an equilibrium strategy depends on whether it is rational for A to depart from that strategy, which in turn depends on how B would react if faced with a departure by A, which in turn depends on how observing A's departure affects B's expectations of A's future moves.

Introducing additional abnormal types of player A is simply an *ad hoc* device to ensure that we never have to address this question, for a departure by A can be interpreted by B as evidence of A's type. By introducing a sufficient number of different abnormal types we can ensure that any possible sequence of moves is an equilibrium sequence for at least one type of A, so that B could never be faced with a logical contradiction. But in an infinitely repeated supergame there is an infinite number of possible strategies, so we would need an infinite number of types to be able to rule out every possible departure from equilibrium by A without confronting B with a logical contradiction.

Unless we are willing to introduce this infinite number of diverse abnormal types we must address the question of how B would react if faced with a logical contradiction between A's conjectured equilibrium strategy and A's actual strategy. It is no answer to say that the question never arises because A will never, in fact, depart from his equilibrium. We cannot know that an equilibrium *is* an equilibrium unless we know what *would* happen if A *were* to depart from equilibrium.

To assume that B would interpret A's departure as a 'mistake' — as the result of A's 'trembling hand' — is not to interpret, but to *fail to interpret* A's departure. It amounts to assuming that B simply ignores a logical contradiction in his belief system between his knowledge of how A will rationally move and his observation of A's actual moves. Instead I propose that we assume that B will maintain if at all possible, and at whatever cost, consistency in his belief system and maintain his hypothesis of A's rationality — that A's moves, whatever they may be, were deliberately chosen and were not 'mistakes'.

Would it be rational for A to depart from a conjectured equilibrium? How would B rationally react to such a departure which presents him with a logical contradiction? If we admit that we do not know the answer to these questions then, paradoxically, our very admission of ignorance is the source of our answer. If we do not know how B would react to A's departure then we also do not know whether it would be rational for A to depart from any conjectured equilibrium. Now if *we*, the theorist, do not know this, then neither does B know whether it would be rational for A to depart from any conjectured equilibrium. But then B *can* interpret A's departure as rational *given* some belief on A's part as to how B would react. B is forced to conjecture A's equilibrium strategy in just the same sense as we are.

If B were to interpret A's play of x^p as a 'mistake', and continue to expect x^d in future, then it would indeed be a mistake. If instead B were to maintain his hypothesis of A's rationality, then he would interpret A's play of x^p as evidence that A believes that B would interpret A's play as rational — as evidence that A expects B to react with y^p — then B would expect A to play x^p in future, would therefore react with y^p, and it would indeed be rational for A to play x^p.

If B were to interpret A's play of x^p as a 'mistake', he would continue to expect A to play x^d in future. It would then indeed be a mistake for A to play x^p, and rational for A to play x^d. Thus B can interpret A's play of x^d as rational if he assumes that A believes that B would interpret a play of x^p as a mistake.

If instead B were to interpret A's play of x^p as rational, he would now expect A to play x^p in future. It would then indeed be rational for A to play x^p, and a mistake for A to play x^d. Thus B can interpret A's play of x^p if he assumes that A believes that B would interpret a play of x^p as rational.

Whether A plays x^p or x^d, B can maintain his hypothesis of A's rationality provided he is willing to adopt a suitable assumption about A's beliefs about B's reactions to A's plays. In other words, provided B maintains his hypothesis of A's rationality, A's play of x^p or x^d *communicates* to B A's beliefs about B's reactions to A's moves.

This is how all communication works. If I wish to communicate the fact that I believe in some proposition P, then I conspicuously perform some action which it would obviously not be rational for me to perform unless I did in fact believe P. Provided my audience maintains its hypothesis of my rationality, my communication succeeds. If instead it interprets my action as a non-rational 'mistake' — the result of an unconscious reflex or 'trembling hand' — then my attempted communication fails.

In some cases of communication, it is not necessary that the audience realizes the speaker's *intention* to communicate for the communication to succeed. For instance, if I wish to communicate my belief that bread is not poisonous, I can do so by simply eating some bread. Provided the audience believe I am not suicidal, the result of my eating bread is to cause them to believe that I believe that bread is not poisonous. They do not need further to assume that I intended to communicate my belief to them to interpret my action as rational. I might simply have been hungry. We can call this sort of communication 'natural' communication.

In other cases of communication, however, it *is* necessary for the audience to realize the speaker's intention to communicate for the communication to succeed. In these cases — which we can call 'symbolic' communication — the speaker communicates his belief only by communicating his *intention* to communicate his belief.[6] An example of symbolic communication is where the manager of a theatre dims the lights in the theatre bar to inform patrons that the next act is about to begin. It is not necessary for the patrons to have been previously informed of the convention that dimmed lights mean the next act will soon begin in order for the communication to succeed. The patrons know that the manager will wish to communicate this fact *somehow*, and momentarily dimming the lights serves as an act of communication precisely because the act is so obviously irrational — unless it can be rationalized as *intended* to seem obviously irrational. This, like other acts of symbolic communication, will fail only if the audience either interprets the act as a 'mistake' (the manager's hand 'trembled' on the light switch), or as rational other than as an act of communication (the manager wished to conserve energy). Dimming the lights succeeds in communicating the manager's intentions precisely because these alternative hypotheses to explain the act are so unlikely. (Consider also waving to a person out of earshot to warn him of danger. This fails if he interprets your arm movement as due to unconscious reflexes, or to a wish to exercise.)

Symbolic communication works by the speaker's performing an action that is obviously deliberate and yet apparently so irrational that the audience can only maintain its hypothesis of the speaker's rationality by assuming that he intended it to be noticed owing to its very apparent irrationality. In symbolic communication what is primarily communicated is no more than the speaker's intention to communicate something. What that something is can either be guessed from the context (what could he want me to believe he believes in these circumstances?) or, eventually, established by convention (he has always uttered the words 'there's a grizzly bear behind you!' in the past when he wants me to believe that he believes that there's a grizzly bear behind me).

Returning to our infinitely repeated game, we see that in playing x^p, A is performing an act of *symbolic* communication. What A wishes to communicate is his belief that it is rational to play x^p. If, by playing x^p, A can get B to believe that A believes that it is rational to play x^p, then B will expect A to play x^p in future and will reply with y^p, as A desires him to do. If instead B fails to understand A's communication, and interprets A's play of x^p as a mistake, then B will play y^d in future, and A's play of x^p will have been a mistake. Acts of *symbolic* communication turn out to be rational, rather than mistakes, only if they are *interpreted* as acts of communication. Acts of *natural* communication, by contrast, can be rational even if the intended audience does not interpret them as intended as acts of communication.

3.4   Conclusion

If we seek an adequate understanding of social institutions, we must see them not as exogenously imposed constraints on agents' actions, but as an aspect of agents' actions themselves. We must see social institutions not as part of the 'rules of the game', but as an outcome of a game that 'brackets', or takes care not to presuppose, society.

I have argued that the 'social' aspect of agents' actions, what it is that qualitatively distinguishes their actions within society from actions in a game against nature, is that the former actions can only be understood as rational if seen as part of a rational rule of action. The examples given at the beginning of this chapter reinforce that argument, for it is hard to imagine any society lacking such elementary examples of social interaction as punishment and exchange, and yet, without an unexplained 'taste' for revenge or rendering a quid pro quo, rational agents would never punish or be deterred by threat of punishment, and would never exchange goods, unless they followed rules of action and expected others too to follow rules of action.

When agents follow rules of action they act as if they had precommitted their actions. But, unlike agents who have actually precommitted, and who are *forced* to carry out their commitments, agents who follow rules *choose* to do so, and stick to their rules of action only because they wish to preserve their reputations for doing so. They carry out their promises only because by doing so, and only by doing so, can they get others to believe their future promises. Now, if an agent's actions were perfectly predictable a priori, reputation would be impossible, for others would then believe that I will, or will not, carry out my future promises regardless of whether I carry out my current promise, so I would have no incentive to keep my current promise, so will break it, as I will break, and be then known to break, future promises. If agents' actions were perfectly predictable a priori then, agents would not rationally follow rules, and so there would be no society.

Wishing to follow rules rationally, yet knowing that he will not rationally do so if his actions were a priori predictable, an agent with free will can and will destroy the supposition of predictability by simply choosing to follow a rule, for in doing so he does something that could not be predicted a priori to be a rational thing for him to do. The rationality of following a rule can only be understood self-referentially — as rational only because intended to appear to have no reason except this very one.

In following a rule an agent communicates that he believes it is rational to follow a rule. This communication is *symbolic* communication, for it can only be understood (can only be interpreted as a rational action) if the audience assumes the intention was to communicate. My speaking fails if others fail to realize that what I am trying to do is speak.

If society is the following of rules, and the following of rules rests on agents' free will, then this explains the otherwise puzzling fact that the set of creatures with whom we believe we could share society coincides with the set of creatures to whom we attribute the moral responsibility of freedom of will.

If society is the following of rules, and the following of rules is an act of symbolic communication, then this also explains the otherwise puzzling fact that we share society with those with whom we can share language.

Notes

1. The problem of time-inconsistency of optimal plans was introduced to economics by Kydland and Prescott (1977), but recognition of what is

essentially the same problem has also appeared in other disciplines. Schelling (1960) considers the rationality of committing oneself to a course of action, which it may appear irrational to carry out *ex post facto*, in order to influence others' expectations of one's future actions. In formal game theory, Selten (1975) introduced the concept of perfect equilibrium in order to restrict equilibrium strategies to those that are, in effect, time consistent. In moral philosophy, Hodgson (1967) uses what is essentially the time-inconsistency problem to argue for rule-utilitarianism against the competing ethical doctrine of act-utilitarianism.

2. This game is a simplified version of the game presented in Kydland and Prescott (1977).

3. In a Stackelberg equilibrium, where A is the 'leader' and B is the 'follower', B chooses his optimal action taking A's action as exogenous, while A chooses his action taking into account the effect of his choice on B's optimal choice. Quite simply, the benefits of precommitment arise because by precommitting A can *choose* his action, and reveal that choice to B, before B chooses, and can thus become a Stackelberg *leader* even though his physical action follows B's action in time.

4. I must add that I am not aware of any explicit statement and acceptance by game theorists of what I call the 'decidability axiom'. Rather, it is my way of interpreting what game theorists are doing.

5. This is strictly correct only if both players have the same information, as is being assumed here. Otherwise, the history of moves might affect subsequent moves by revealing information about the players' preferences and beliefs.

6. See, for instance, Grice (1969).

4

The State of Nature

4.1 Introduction

The central question of this book is to explain the nature and
existence of social institutions from the economic perspective of
rational individualism. What are social institutions? Why do they
exist? In Chapter 2 I proposed an answer — social institutions are
identical to agents following rules of action, and agents rationally
follow rules of action because doing so enables them to influence
other agents' expectations of their actions.

The best defence I can give for my thesis is one by example —
showing that this answer can provide a plausible account of the
nature and existence of *particular* social institutions. In this chapter
I consider the institution of private property rights as an example of
a social institution — an example chosen primarily because of its
obvious relevance to economics. Nearly all economic theorizing is
conducted under the explicit or implicit assumption of an exogenously given institution of private property rights. The very objects
of analysis in the theory of exchange, for example, are not physically defined objects, but agents' *rights* to behave in certain ways
with respect to various objects.

We must keep in mind, however, when seeking to explain the
nature and existence of property rights, that this particular social
institution has been chosen only as an *example* to represent social
institutions in general. What is at issue is not the existence of one

particular social institution, but the existence of *any* social institutions. Our explanation of property rights must not, in this case, presuppose the existence of any other social institutions. For example, if we were to explain private property rights as resulting from government legislation, or as evolving from an initial situation of common property rights, without also explaining the existence of the social institutions of government or of common property, we should have failed in our task. Our task is to examine the logical compatibility between the existence of property rights and the economic approach of rational individualism. To assume some pre-existing social institutions would be to beg the question, for how could we know that *those* institutions could be accounted for from our individualistic perspective? Just as a *partial* equilibrium theory of prices explains some prices by taking other prices as given, and a *general* equilibrium theory explains all prices simultaneously, so we seek not a partial, but a general equilibrium theory of social institutions.

4.2   The Methodological Role of the State of Nature

We seek to answer two questions. What are property rights? Why do property rights exist?

The first question is one of conceptual analysis, as much a philosophical as an economic question. To understand this question, we must imagine ourselves as anthropologists, discovering a previously unknown group of agents. Under what circumstances would we be logically justified in saying that those agents were participants in a social institution of property rights? What sorts of actions and what sorts of beliefs on the part of those agents would constitute their having a system of property rights? If we could not even give an individualistic account of what it *means* to say that property rights exist, then an individualistic account of social institutions would be sheer nonsense.

The second question is more a question of economic theory in the narrower sense. If a group of agents performing certain sorts of actions and holding certain sorts of beliefs constitutes their having a system of property rights, then why do individual agents rationally perform those actions and hold those beliefs?

We will attempt to answer both questions within the context of a single conceptual experiment. The conceptual experiment is that of imagining an initial 'State of Nature' of completely asocial agents, and explaining why a system of private property rights might spontaneously develop from this initial position.

In positing an 'initial' State of Nature and discussing the 'development' of social institutions in this State of Nature, we are *not* implying that the State of Nature existed as a historical fact, nor are we saying that the historical development of social institutions took place in this manner. What we are doing is not historical analysis, but performing a *stability experiment*.

A stability experiment is a way of explaining why things are the way they are. We imagine things being different from the way they are, and show that if they *were* different then there would exist forces tending to restore things to the way they are now.

Suppose we wished to explain why the level of water in Lake Ontario is the same on the Canadian side of the border as it is on the United States side.[1] An explanation by way of a stability experiment would run as follows. Imagine that divine intervention were to bring about an 'initial position' in which the water level on the Canadian side of the border were higher than on the US side. This state of affairs could not persist after divine intervention were removed, for the pressure of water on the Canadian side would exceed that on the US side, and water would flow from the former to the latter, thereby reducing the disparity in levels. That is why, in the absence of divine intervention, we never see a disparity of levels.

Stability experiments are not uncommon in economics. Hume (1742) performs a stability experiment when he imagines a magical annihilation of part of the money supply in a small open economy on the gold standard. He uses this conceptual experiment to elucidate the workings of the price–specie flow mechanism in restoring the money supply to its original level. Patinkin (1965) does the same when he posits an arbitrary increase in the price level, which he uses to elucidate the operation of the real balance effect in restoring the original price level.

In each case, the stability experiment is used to show that a particular variable is endogenous, and its level is determined in equilibrium by other, exogenous, variables. To show this, the theorist posits a purely *arbitrary*, or 'magical', change in the endogenous variable while holding the exogenous variables constant. He then shows, *holding that endogenous variable at its new level by theorist's fiat*, there would exist forces which, if permitted to operate, would tend to restore that variable to its original level. In positing an 'initial position' in which the endogenous variable is at a 'wrong' or *disequilibrium* level, relative to the exogenous variables, the theorist is certainly not saying that such a state of affairs ever existed at some historical time. On the contrary, the whole point of the stability experiment is to demonstrate that such a state of affairs could not, in fact, exist.

Similarly, in positing a State of Nature in which no social institutions exist, we are not saying that the State of Nature is a historical reality. The only point of positing its existence is to explain its non-existence. We seek to show that the existence of social institutions is endogenously determined by some exogenous attribute of the world, and do so by showing that the State of Nature — a state of affairs with the *same* exogenous attributes as the actual world, but with no social institutions — is a *disequilibrium* state of affairs.

This is not to deny that at some time or place some (or even all) social institutions might not exist, any more than Hume or Patinkin would deny that the money supply or price level respectively might be different at some time or place from what they are here and now. It is instead to argue that if the endogenous variable were in fact different at some other time or place, it would have to result from different values of the exogenous variables. If our analysis is successful, an actual state of affairs in which property rights did not exist could not be the State of Nature, for the latter, as we seek to show, is a state of affairs in which the absence of property rights is inappropriate or impossible given the exogenous circumstances.

The exogenous circumstances of the State of Nature are meant to represent, albeit abstractly, those of here and now. There is nothing wrong, for example (though we do not do this), in positing a State of Nature with a highly developed technology and stock of capital. The State of Nature is not an historical fact but an ever-present logical possibility.[2] In speaking of the 'emergence' or 'development' of social institutions we are not discussing some historical process. We are elucidating the forces which *maintain the existence* of the current set of social institutions.

We need to examine the State of Nature in some detail to examine the forces therein which would lead to the emergence of property rights and hence a dissolution of the State of Nature. To do this, we place an *arbitrary constraint* on the behaviour of agents to prevent them taking the sorts of actions which would constitute their establishment of property rights. What we seek to show is that rational agents would wish to violate that arbitrarily imposed constraint. The State of Nature will therefore be examined as a *constrained equilibrium* — an equilibrium given the arbitrary constraint on agents' behaviour. But since the imposition of that constraint is purely arbitrary, if agents wished to violate that constraint then the State of Nature would in fact be a disequilibrium state of affairs, which is what we seek to prove. If we can show that rational individual agents would indeed wish to violate the arbitrary constraint which prevents their establishing property rights, then we will *ipso facto* have explained why property rights exist.

Our strategy must be slightly more oblique than this, however, for we seek to explain not only the existence, but also the nature, of property rights. If we do not yet know what sorts of action and belief would constitute their having a system of property rights, we do not know what arbitrary constraint to impose on agents to preserve the State of Nature as a constrained equilibrium. We resolve this problem as follows. The constraint will be imposed implicitly, and revealed later. We will simply posit a State of Nature in which agents behave in a manner which resembles our intuitive conception of a world without property rights. We will then suggest an alternative course of action which rational agents would choose to take and which, if taken, would lead instead to a different state of affairs, the 'Social Equilibrium', which resembles our intuitive conception of a world with property rights. The constraint we would need to impose to preserve the State of Nature as a constrained equilibrium will then simply be the prohibition of that alternative course of action which, if taken, would lead to the Social Equilibrium — a world with property rights. In discovering which sorts of actions the theorist would need to prohibit to prevent the Social

Equilibrium from being the outcome, we will simultaneously have discovered the nature of the actions and associated expectations which constitute the social institution of property rights.

3.3   The State of Nature

Skogh and Stuart (1982) have already presented a useful model of the State of Nature. I will use their model here, adding two interesting extensions of my own.

All agents are identical. Each has a fixed amount of a scarce resource, his own time or labour, which he can allocate between three mutually exclusive activities. The first activity is the *production* of goods, the consumption of which yields utility. Time devoted to the second activity, *transfer*, enables the agent to consume goods produced by other agents. Time devoted to the third activity, *protection*, reduces the quantity of goods transferred to other agents, for a given amount of transfer activity on their part. The three activities are neither pleasurable nor unpleasurable in themselves, only for the consumption they provide. For substance we can think of the goods as bananas, with agents spending their time producing bananas, transferring bananas by searching for bananas grown by other agents, or protecting the bananas grown by concealing them from search by other agents. From our own perspective as participants in a social institution of private property rights, we naturally tend to think of an agent as *owning* the bananas that he has produced (unless he has renounced that right by contract), and think of transfer activity as *stealing*, but these concepts are not meaningful in the State of Nature. We will, however, refer to the goods an agent has produced as 'his' goods, merely as a convenient shorthand.

We assume that in any given year agents choose their allocations of time simultaneously, in ignorance of the allocations chosen by other agents. An agent's utility in any year depends only on his consumption of goods in that year, which in turn is the sum of his production of goods, plus net transfers of goods from other agents. (We assume that goods are perishable and so cannot be stored from one year to the next.) I define the State of Nature to be the Nash equilibrium to the single year's game — each agent allocates his time between the three activities so as to maximize his utility, taking as given the allocations chosen by other agents. We will assume that preferences and technology are such as to yield a unique interior equilibrium. This requires that there be sufficiently decreasing returns to each activity that an agent who maximizes his consumption by dividing his time between the three activities so as to equalize their marginal returns spends a strictly positive amount of time in each. In equilibrium, since aggregate consumption equals aggregate production, and all agents are identical, each agent's consumption will equal his production of goods.

The State of Nature is inefficient in the following sense. The prohibition of transfer activity by dictatorial fiat, since this would also eliminate agents' incentives to engage in protection activity, would mean that all time would now be devoted to production, and hence each agent's consumption and utility would increase. Time devoted to transfer and protection, though profitable from the point of view of an individual agent, imposes an external cost on other agents, whose consumption is reduced. Conflict over the distribution of resources is costly in aggregate because it diverts resources away from production and so reduces aggregate consumption.

Two simple extensions to the model described above can reveal additional sources of inefficiency.

The first extension is to introduce an additional good which is harder to transfer and easier to protect than the first good. An example might be leisure, which we might suppose to be nontransferable. Agents reap the full returns to 'producing' leisure, but only part of the returns to producing bananas, and so will devote too much time to leisure relative to producing bananas. An individual agent who spent more time producing bananas and less on leisure, other things equal, would create external benefits, for other agents would now enjoy higher net transfers of bananas.

With this first extension, the efficiency losses due to transfer activity in the State of Nature are embarrassingly similar to the efficiency losses usually attributed to a proportional or progressive income tax.[3] Some resources are used up in collecting the tax (transfer activity). Some resources are used up in tax evasion (protection activity). There is a misallocation of resources away from taxable activities (producing bananas) towards untaxed activities (leisure).

So far, all that is required to ensure an efficient allocation of resources is a prohibition of transfer activity. This result is not general, and does not hold if we make a second extension of the model.

Let us introduce a third good, 'apples', which, like bananas, are transferable. Assume that agents are identical with respect to preferences and transfer and protection technologies, but that type A agents have a comparative advantage in producing apples, while type B agents have a comparative advantage in producing bananas.

Obviously, the mere prohibition of transfer activity now no longer ensures an efficient allocation of resources, for this would restrict agents to self-sufficiency, whereas efficiency requires that type A agents specialize in producing apples, while type B agents specialize in producing bananas, while both types consume both goods. Indeed, under some parameter values the prohibition of transfer activity would make agents worse off than in the State of Nature. To see this, notice that type A agents will devote more time to the transfer and protection of bananas than will type B agents, since the alternative way of increasing consumption of bananas — by producing more — is less rewarding for type A agents than for type B agents. Similarly, type B agents will devote more time to the transfer and protection of apples than will type A agents. Therefore, in the State of Nature there will be net transfers of bananas from type B to type A agents, and net transfers of apples from type A to type B agents. Now make the extreme assumption that type A agents can produce *no* bananas, and that type B agents can produce *no* apples, and that consumption of *both* apples and bananas is required to support life. A prohibition of transfer activity would, under these extreme assumptions, condemn agents to death, whereas they could survive in the State of Nature. It therefore follows that a mere prohibition of transfer activity could make agents worse off than in the State of Nature.

In the absence of voluntary exchange, forced exchange may be Pareto Improving, for each agent will tend to 'steal' that type of good he values more highly. Forced exchange is inefficient relative to voluntary exchange, however, since under forced exchange resources are devoted not only to effect *but also to prevent* a transfer of goods, whereas under voluntary exchange no resources are used to prevent transfer, so that more resources are used under forced than under voluntary exchange for a given net transfer of goods.

4.4   Functionalism

One approach to the study of social institutions, which I have called Functionalism, views social institutions as a set of constraints on agents' behaviour (much like physical barriers), asserts that the actual social institutions will be those that are most efficient, and asserts that to demonstrate the efficiency of a social institution suffices to explain its existence. I have criticized this approach in Chapter 2, but it is nevertheless worthwhile to examine what a Functionalist account of social institutions would look like in the context of our model of the State of Nature.

Let us imagine someone building a matrix of unclimbable fences in our world of the original position, and placing one agent within each compound. These fences would obviously eliminate transfer activity, and would thus also eliminate the incentives to agents to devote time to protection activity. Each agent would then devote all his time to production (of bananas, apples, and leisure) within his own compound. Before we introduced the second transferable good, apples, this would have ensured an efficient allocation of resources, but once apples are introduced it would no longer do so. We would have to modify the fences by introducing a clever little device called an 'exchange mechanism'. An exchange mechanism is a pair of boxes, one on each side of the fence. Goods (apples and bananas) can be placed in each box, and if both agents pull a lever simultaneously the boxes swivel to the opposite sides of the fence, so that each agent gets control of the goods that the other agent had placed in the box.

These fences and exchange mechanisms provide an exact mechanical counterpart to the social institution of private alienable property rights. Property rights (the fences) are exogenously defined and inviolable. Each agent can, however, voluntarily give up his rights to another agent, by using the exchange mechanism, contingent on the other agent giving up some of his rights in exchange. We could even use this mechanical counterpart to represent the costs of enforcing property rights, by supposing that the fences need maintenance, and represent transactions costs by supposing that it requires effort to pull the levers on the exchange mechanisms. (I confess I have no idea how to contruct a mechanical counterpart for intertemporal exchange or for exchange of services, however.)

If the State of Nature corresponds to a world without property rights, and if the presence of fences and exchange mechanisms corresponds to a world with property rights, then we have revealed the inefficiency of the allocation of resources in a world without property rights relative to a world with property rights. In doing this, however, we have *not* explained either the nature or the existence of property rights.

The fences and exchange mechanisms are an obvious *deus ex machina* brought in to save the agents from their predicament in the State of Nature. Our imposing fences and exchange mechanisms does not create property rights; it merely changes the physical constraints facing agents in such a way that property rights become unnecessary. Each agent has become a Robinson Crusoe: his compound, his island. The fences and exchange mechanisms are clearly a fiction, but then why should agents not treat them as such, and simply ignore them? It is true that if *all* agents were to act *as if* the fences and exchange mechanisms existed then all agents would be better off, but it would be a violation of the individualistic approach (a fallacy of composition in reverse) if we were to conclude from this that *each* individual agent would therefore act as if fences and exchange mechanisms existed. Taking as given other agents' decisions whether to act as if the fences existed, each individual agent is better off acting as if they did not exist.

The social contract can be understood as a promise by each agent to act as if the fences existed in exchange for a similar promise by other agents, but the fact that all agents would *like* to participate in such a contract does not mean that they *can* do so. To assume that they *can* do so is to assume the existence of the social institution of contract, thus begging the question we seek to answer — how social institutions can exist in a world of self-seeking rational individuals. If the social contract enforces property rights, how is the social contract enforced? We have simply replaced one game of Prisoner's Dilemma with another.

The Functionalist approach is a red herring. What we need to explain is why each individual agent would choose to act *as if* the fences existed, even though they do not exist.

4.5   Why is the State of Nature Asocial?

I have defined the State of Nature to be the Nash equilibrium of the model described in section 4.3 — the allocation of resources that results when each agent maximizes his utility, taking as given the actions of other agents. What justifies our saying that property rights are absent in this state of affairs? What is the qualitative distinction between agents' behaviour in the State of Nature and their behaviour in a world with property rights?

The mere fact that agents engage in transfer and protection activity does not differentiate the State of Nature from the actual world, where property rights exist. Agents in the actual world also devote resources to 'transfer' — to enable the goods produced by one agent to be consumed by another. (Some of this transfer activity is legal: the resources used up in transport and exchange between producer and consumer; and some of it is illegal: the resources used by thieves.) Agents in the actual world also devote resources to 'protection'. The difference lies, however, in the *ways* that agents protect goods.

In the State of Nature agents protect goods by actions which they undertake *before or simultaneously with* the transfer activity they wish to counter. There exists a *purely technological relationship* between the level of protection activity and the amount of transfers *for a given amount of transfer activity*. We see agents in the actual world use similar sorts of actions to protect goods from theft, such as concealing goods, installing physical barriers, and posting guards with power sufficient to prevent goods being taken. But these are not the only ways, nor the main ways in which agents protect goods. It is a relatively quick and simple matter to learn the skills necessary to circumvent the locks on a vehicle, and it is far cheaper to gain physical possession of a vehicle by stealing one than by earning the money needed to buy one. But then why do agents in the actual world not reallocate their time away from production (earning the money to buy cars), into transfer (stealing cars) where the marginal returns are obviously so much higher? The answer, of course, (at least from the economist's perspective) is that most people do not steal cars largely because they fear the consequences — that if their action is discovered not only will they lose physical possession of the stolen car, but they will also suffer punishment.

Deterrence is the primary method of protection in the actual world. Other devices, such as fences and locks, are used only to the extent that identification and apprehension of the criminal, and hence the imposition of punishment, is costly or impossible. The fundamental difference between deterrence and other methods of protection is that deterrence works by creating an *expectation* on the part of a potential thief that an act of transfer will induce a *subsequent* change in behaviour of the victim (or his allies) that will reduce the *future utility* of the thief. The *act* of punishing, which takes place *after* the good has been transferred, is not what prevents the transfer. It is the prior *expectation* of this act which prevents the transfer, and it does so only by inducing a potential thief to *choose to devote fewer resources to transfer activity*. The efficacy of deterrence, unlike other methods of protecting goods, is not a purely technological matter.

The use of deterrence implies that the user views his opponent as *rational*. He seeks to modify the opponent's *expectations* so as to modify his *rational choice*. You cannot deter a non-rational opponent, only one with expectations and preferences. Rocks and plants are quite unaffected by fear of the consequences. Other methods of protection do not require that the opponent be viewed as rational. The concealment of goods, and the construction of physical barriers, are equally effective against both rational and non-rational predators.

This is what justifies our claim that property rights do not exist in the State of Nature. A collection of agents, each of whom perceives himself as being the *only* rational agent, cannot be said to constitute a society — cannot be said to partake in any social institution — for each acts as if he were Robinson Crusoe playing a game against nature. Agents in the State of Nature, failing to use deterrence, protect goods from other agents in fundamentally the same way as they would protect goods from non-rational predators. Acting thus, it would be totally redundant for them to ascribe rationality to other agents. In other words, they act as if each believes himself to be a solitary rational agent, and so they cannot be said to have a system of property rights, nor indeed to participate in any social institution. If instead they were to use deterrence, each would thereby be recognizing the existence of other rational agents, fulfilling a necessary condition for their being said to constitute a society.

4.6   Escaping the State of Nature

So far we have provided a model of the State of Nature, and have argued that the social institution of property rights does not exist in the State of Nature, since each agent acts as if he were the only rational agent.

If we are to explain the existence of property rights we must show that the State of Nature is *not* in fact an equilibrium state of affairs — that the allocation we have called the State of Nature would *not* in fact be the outcome of rational individual behaviour under the postulated preferences and technology of the original position. In other words, we must now show that our prediction of how agents would behave in that situation is *false*. If the outcome of rational individual behaviour were, in fact, the misery of the State of Nature then rational individuals must remain in that state of misery. No *deus ex machina*, such as fences and exchange mechanisms or collective action in pursuit of collective goals, can be brought in to save them. They must either escape the State of Nature by their own *individual* efforts, or there they must remain.

What mistake might I, the theorist, have made in analysing the agents' behaviour? What mistakes are our agents making when they act as they do in the State of Nature? How are they behaving irrationally? The mistake made by each agent in the State of Nature is that he lets bygones be bygones. He fails to follow an 'historical' strategy in which his current action depends irreducibly upon past events. He fails to follow a *rule of action*. In failing to do these things, he fails to exploit his ability to influence the actions of other agents by influencing their expectations of his future actions.

Our specification of agents' preferences and technology in the original position contained no way in which the outcome of the game in one year could influence the situation facing agents in subsequent years. It seemed, therefore, that we could consider each year in isolation from previous and subsequent years. Doing so serves to rule out historical strategies, and eliminates the possibility of agents' following rules of action, since they all move only once and simultaneously.

Now the theory of rational behaviour I have called act-individualism implies that it is legitimate to treat each year in isolation in these circumstances, which means that if act-individualism were true then the State of Nature would indeed be the equilibrium allocation and property rights would not exist. Under the alternative theory of rational behaviour, which I have called rule-individualism, it is not legitimate to treat each year in isolation, since individual agents could gain by following rules of action which specify current actions contingent on the behaviour of other agents in previous years.

The sort of historical strategy I have in mind is a deterrence strategy. An agent would follow a rule of action in which he punished his opponent in the current year contingent on how his opponent acted towards him in the previous year. We do not need to modify the exogenous parameters of the original position to make deterrence strategies possible. The assumed preferences and technology already contain possibilities for agents to punish and reward the actions of other agents, provided they can observe the actions of other agents after the event, and provided they can direct their transfer and protection activities against specific other agents. If agent A observes that agent B engages in transfer activity against A's goods in year one, then A can punish B by engaging in large amounts of transfer activity against B in year two. If, on the other hand, A instead observes that B engages in no transfer activity against A in year one, then A can reward B by engaging in no transfer activity against B in year two.

Faced with A's following this sort of historical strategy, how would B rationally react? When considering the amount of transfer activity he will direct against goods produced by A, B would take into account not only the effect on his current consumption (as he does in the State of Nature), but also the effect on his future consumption that results if his current transfer activity triggers retaliation by A. Knowing that A is following this sort of historical strategy would modify B's incentives, leading him rationally to choose a lower level of transfer activity against A's goods. Indeed, it will presumably be feasible for A to impose a stiff enough penalty to deter B completely from engaging in transfer activity against A's goods.

Suppose that it were possible for A to follow a strategy which, if B believed A to be following that strategy, would completely deter B from transferring A's goods. Would it be rational for A to do so?

If we adopt the perspective of act-individualism, which maintains that rationality pertains to each action in isolation, then it could never be rational for A to act thus. By definition, as an act-individualist A ignores the effect of his method of choosing actions upon the expectations and behaviour of other agents. It is not the act of punishment itself, but B's expectation of that act, which benefits A. In year one, A would like B to believe that A's action in year two will depend on B's action in year one. When year two arrives however, A will reformulate his optimal plan, this time taking B's action in year one as parametric, since it is past and hence unalterable. What B did in year one has no effect on the situation facing A in year two, so that A's optimal discretionary action for year two, chosen in year two, is independent of B's action in year one. For a rational act-individualist, bygones are forever bygones, and so he will never follow a deterrence strategy in which current actions depend irreducibly on past events.

If instead we adopt the perspective of rule-individualism, then it could be rational for A to follow a rule in which A completely deters B from transferring A's goods. To see this, suppose that A and B are identical, and compare A's utility under the deterrence strategy with A's utility under his strategy in the State of Nature.

In the State of Nature, since both are identical, they will engage in identical amounts of transfer (and protection) activity, and so there will be zero net transfers of goods between A and B. Under the deterrence strategy, B will be deterred from transfer activity against A, and so A will not need to punish B in equilibrium, and so A will not engage in transfer activity against B. Thus in this case too there will be no net transfers of goods between A and B. The difference between the two cases is that under the deterrence strategy, since A will not be devoting time to transfer (nor to protection) activity against B, A will have extra time available to devote to production (or to transfer and protection against other agents) and so will have higher consumption and hence higher utility than in the State of Nature.

Thus A can gain by following, and being believed to follow, a rule whereby he deters B from transferring A's goods. From the perspective of rule-individualism, the rationality of an action cannot be assessed without reference to the rule of action of which it is a part. It is not the isolated action of punishment or reward which deters B, but B's belief that A is following a rule of punishment and reward. A would be irrational to choose any level of transfer and protection other than that which maximizes his current consumption, irrespective of B's past actions, taking as given B's belief that A's future actions will conform to that rule. The only reason A can have for performing particular acts of punishment or reward is that his failure to do so would result in the loss of his reputation for doing so — B would drop his belief that A was following that rule of action. Provided the future costs to A of thus losing his reputation would outweigh his immediate benefits from departing from his rule, he will not rationally depart from his rule.

If act-individualism is the correct theory of rational action, therefore, A would not rationally follow a deterrence strategy (nor therefore would B rationally expect him to do so), and so the institutionless State of Nature would indeed be the equilibrium outcome of the original position. This example therefore illustrates and supports my thesis that act-individualism is logically incompatible with the existence of social institutions. On the other hand, if rule-individualism is correct, A might rationally choose to follow a deterrence strategy, which involves a departure from his postulated behaviour in the State of Nature, and so the outcome we called the State of Nature would not, in fact, be an equilibrium state of affairs.

The arbitrary constraint that we implicitly imposed on agents' behaviour, which must be imposed if the State of Nature is to be preserved as a constrained equilibrium, was to prohibit agents from following rules of action. The 'mistake' made by agents in the State of Nature (or the 'mistake' I made in predicting their behaviour in the original position) is to fail to take into account the effect of their method of choosing actions on the expectations and hence behaviour of other agents. Agents in the State of Nature fail to follow rules of action, and their failure to do so is not rational.

4.7 The Social Equilibrium

When agent A follows a deterrence strategy against agent B, and B learns that A is doing so, neither will engage in transfer activity against the other, and so neither will need to engage in protection activity against the other. They act *as if* there were an unclimbable fence between them. They act *as if* they had signed a contract in which each renounces engaging in transfer activity against the other in exchange for a similar renunciation by the other. A Functionalist would reach the same conclusion, but he would justify this conclusion merely on the grounds that *both* are better off if *both* act thus, than if *both* acted as in the State of Nature. I justify this conclusion on the grounds that *each* is better off if *he* acts thus, than if *he* acted as in the State of Nature.

Just as the following of rules can ensure an allocation in which agents act as if there were an unclimbable fence between them (an autarkic allocation), so too can the following of (different) rules support an allocation in which agents act as if the fences incorporated the devices I have called exchange mechanisms (an exchange allocation). In voluntary exchange, B transfers some of A's goods without A engaging in protection activity to hinder that transfer and without A punishing B for having taken A's goods. For an exchange allocation to be possible there must be some gesture which A can make (pulling the lever of an imaginary exchange mechanism), which tells B that his transfer of these goods from A will not trigger subsequent punishment by A. What gives this gesture meaning is A's following a rule of punishing B's transfer activity when A has not made this gesture, and refraining from punishing B when A has made this gesture. It is A's following this rule, and being known to do so, which gives an otherwise irrelevant movement of A's arm the power of a symbol — making the gesture constitutes the giving of A's consent to B's taking his goods. His rule of action having given his gesture its meaning, A can then use his power to give consent to the taking of his goods to induce another agent to render a quid pro quo. Thus, providing the normal conditions for the efficiency of exchange are met (as they are when agents differ in their relative abilities to produce apples and bananas), A does better by following a rule which enables him to give his consent to the taking of his goods, than by following a simpler rule in which all transfers are punished.

The State of Nature is a Nash equilibrium in *actions* — each individual agent chooses his *actions* rationally given the *actions* chosen by other agents. The Social Equilibrium is a Nash equilibrium in *rules of action* — each individual agent chooses his *rule of action* rationally, taking as given the rules of action (if any) followed by other agents, and otherwise taking into account how his chosen rule of action will affect the rational choices of action by other agents.

An outside observer, who did not understand the social institution of private property rights, would find the behaviour of agents in the Social Equilibrium very puzzling. He would observe agents engaging in no protection activity, so there would be no physical barriers to inhibit transfer activity. The whole of an agent's produce apparently would be completely vulnerable to other agents' transfer activity. He would observe *some* transfer activity, but it would be peculiarly limited, both in scope and in kind. Apple-producing agents would only transfer bananas, and banana-producing agents would only transfer apples, and neither type would transfer as much of the good as would seem rational. Why would agents be seen to devote considerable time and effort to *producing* apples or bananas when physically identical apples or bananas (those produced by other agents) could simply be *taken*, with negligible expenditure of time and effort? Why do agents' actions, in other words, fail to correspond to merely the *physical* barriers and constraints of their *natural* environment?

Faced with such puzzling behaviour, our outside observer might postulate an *imaginary* set of physical barriers to supplement the actual physical barriers. Even though fences and exchange mechanisms do not in fact exist, it is possible to explain and predict agents' behaviour by assuming that they do exist. Agents behave *as if* there were unclimbable fences and exchange mechanisms separating each agent. (Alternatively, he might postulate a system of taboos — agents behave *as if* they disliked consuming the goods produced by other agents, except when the producing agent performs the magical gesture which lifts the taboo against another agent consuming his goods.) Seen in this light, social institutions are none other than theoretical constructs, or fictional entities, adopted by both social agents and social theorists alike, which enable them to make sense of agents' behaviour *within* an exogenously given framework of social institutions.

It is this lack of correspondence between agents' actions and the merely physical constraints of their natural environment, and the consequent temptation to postulate additional imaginary 'social constraints' on their behaviour, which justifies our claim that agents in the Social Equilibrium recognize a social institution — that property rights exist in the Social Equilibrium. Each agent recognizes the bygone *physical fact* of past production as entailing the *social fact* of the producing agent's current *ownership* of those goods. Similarly, each agent recognizes the physical fact of a particular sort of movement of an agent's arm (pulling the lever of an imaginary exchange mechanism) as constituting the social fact of ceding his right of ownership to another — a pair of such gestures constituting the social fact of the exchange of property rights.

What enables these physical facts to count as social facts — what gives them the *meaning* that they have — are the rules of action that agents follow and believe others to be following. If we ask why agents obey not only physical constraints but also the hypothetical 'social constraints', we must refer to the beliefs each agent holds regarding the likely effects of his violation of those imaginary constraints upon the expectations and future actions of other agents, and these in turn depend on the rules of action which agents follow and are believed to follow. An agent will not violate another's property rights because he fears the consequences of his doing so on other agents' beliefs about the rule of action he is following, and fears the consequences of his doing so upon the future actions of other agents given the rules of action he believes them to be following. In saying that an agent does not steal because he fears both punishment and loss of trust we make implicit reference to the following of rules of action. The anticipated penalties for violation of the 'rules of the game' which define action within a given framework of social institutions, and are taken as exogenous to the game within that framework, are themselves endogenous to the broader pre-social game, and are created by the rules of action rationally adopted by individual agents playing that broader game.

4.8   A Gloss on the Preceding

The difference between the State of Nature and the Social Equilibrium is that agents follow rules of action in the latter and do not do so in the former. The rationale for following rules of action is that an agent who does so can thereby influence other agents' expectations of his future behaviour. In a game against blind nature, which does not have expectations, the following of rules is therefore without rationale. Conversely, the following of rules implies that the rule-follower thereby recognizes the existence of other rational agents — that he is not playing a game against blind nature. In failing to follow rules, agents in the State of Nature fail to attribute rationality to other agents — they act as if they were solitary, and it is this that makes the State of Nature asocial. Conversely, in following rules, agents in the Social Equilibrium attribute rationality to other agents, and it is this that makes the Social Equilibrium truly social — which makes it legitimate to say that the social institution of property rights exists when agents behave in that way. Ultimately therefore, the question of the existence of social institutions is the question of agents' mutual recognition of each other's rationality — of their decisions to conceive of each other as people, rather than as things. To explain the emergence of society is to explain the recognition of intersubjectivity.

The agents with whom we populated the initial position are

initially solipsists — each thinking of himself as the only mind in existence. We can imagine this by taking a number of Robinson Crusoes, each having played a lonely game against nature on his own isolated island, and placing them all together on a single 'crowded' island, where their actions cannot but impinge on each other. How will these agents come to recognize the rationality of other agents?

The consequences of any plan of action, and hence the utility an agent can attain by implementing that plan, depend on the constraints facing him — on how the 'rest of the world' responds to his actions. Hence it will generally benefit an agent to invest resources in collecting information about those constraints, so that he can formulate his optimal plan taking that information into account, and thereby increase his expected utility. The agents we have placed in the initial position, in other words, will want to learn about the world they inhabit in order to discover the consequences of different actions in order to discover the best actions to take.

Part of the world facing an agent will be nature. He will want to predict nature's 'behaviour'. (If he plants seeds in spring, will nature respond by growing fruit?) Part of the world facing an agent will be the behaviour of other agents. (If the seeds bear fruit, will another creature respond by eating that fruit?) If the constraints facing an agent include the behaviour of another agent, it may benefit him to collect information on the determinants of that behaviour, the better to predict and control it. The agent we have placed in the initial position will be, like us, a theorist. He will need to construct a theory of his environment, which will include a theory of human behaviour.

If we assume that it is rational for us, as economists, to construct a theory of human behaviour by positing a set of preferences and beliefs, and attributing rationality to our subjects, then it seems reasonable to assume that it would also be rational for an agent in the initial position to do likewise, when he constructs a theory of the behaviour of other agents in the initial position.

Now there is no reason why one cannot attribute preferences and beliefs to non-humans as well, not merely to non-human animals but also to inanimate objects, and explain their behaviour as the result of maximizing utility given their beliefs. Extreme behaviourists and extreme primitives apart, we often find it useful to do so for some animals, but not for rocks and plants. But when we ascribe full-fledged rationality, as we do of normal human beings, we are doing something more than this. In choosing to attribute rationality in the full sense of the word, we choose to model the other as being like ourselves — we predict his behaviour in given circumstances by asking ourselves what we would do in those same circumstances (assuming roughly comparable preferences). We can understand his behaviour in that we can imagine ourselves behaving in the same way if we were in his shoes. It is our ability to do this which makes the hypothesis of another's rationality so powerful as a method of understanding and predicting his behaviour. (And to the extent that the other is sufficiently different from ourselves that we cannot accurately predict his behaviour by imagining ourselves in his shoes, so too does the ascription of rationality lose its power relative to other types of theories.)[4]

In adopting the hypothesis that another is rational, in the full sense of the word, we thereby hypothesize his being on the same epistemological footing as ourselves. If *we* can construct theories, then so can *he*. In ascribing rationality to another, we *ipso facto* recognize his ability in turn to ascribe rationality to ourselves. If it is rational for us to construct a theory of the other's behaviour in which we posit his rationality, then it is rational to assume that he will construct a theory of our behaviour in which he posits our rationality, if he is in a similar situation with respect to us as we are to him. So the agent in the initial position who, needing a theory to predict and control the behaviour of another, decides to attribute rationality to the other, at the same time recognizes that the other will similarly be seeking to construct a theory of his behaviour, and will similarly attribute rationality to him. In this manner, the rationality of both agents may become common knowledge between both agents.

Mutual recognition of rationality fundamentally alters the game played by the agents. Each is now playing a game not against blind nature, but against another rational agent whose moves depend on the theory he holds about other players' likely moves. The utility that A can attain in this game depends upon B's moves, which in turn depend upon B's theory of how A will move. A can thus have an *incentive* to modify B's theory about A, since doing so will affect B's moves which in turn affect A's utility. A also has an *ability* to modify B's theory since, possessing free will, he is able, if he so chooses, to contradict any theory B might hold about A's moves, and thereby force B to abandon his thus falsified theory. What this means is that there exists no theory of A's actions which is true independent of A's wanting that theory to be believed as true.

We must therefore distinguish two types or levels of theory about a rational agent's behaviour. The first, or lower level theory, correctly predicts an agent's actions when that agent ignores his ability to modify that theory — when he takes as given other agents' theories of his actions. This theory corresponds to what I have called act-individualism, and describes how agents behave in the State of Nature. The second, or higher level theory, correctly predicts an agent's actions when that agent takes into account his ability to modify that theory — when he takes as endogenous other agents' theories of his actions. This theory corresponds to what I have called rule-individualism, and describes how agents behave in the Social Equilibrium.

4.9   Conclusion

What I have done in this chapter is to provide an account of the nature and existence of a particular social institution, that of private property rights, based on rational individual behaviour. I have used property rights as an example to illustrate the central thesis of this book that it is possible to provide an account of social institutions from the methodological approach which assumes rational individual behaviour, but only if we shift our attention from the rationality of *actions* to the rationality of *rules of action*. Act-individualism leads to the institutionless State of Nature, where each agent acts as if he were the only rational agent. Rule-individualism leads to the Social Equilibrium, where agents recognize and respect property rights. The reason why life in the State of Nature is 'nasty, brutish, and short' is that the agents therein fail to follow rules of action — they fail to exploit their ability to influence other agents' expectations of their future behaviour.

It is not for us, the theorists, to rescue agents from their predicament in the State of Nature by invoking the various *dei ex machina*, the collective Leviathans, the social contracts, the Functionalist fallacies of composition. If they are methodologically committed to rational individualism, then, if rational individual agents choose actions which result in the State of Nature, they are stuck there. If rational individual behaviour did indeed lead to the State of Nature, one must either reject rational individualism or else (implausibly) accept that the world we inhabit, despite appearances to the contrary, is in fact the State of Nature, and society an illusion by which rational agents are inexplicably fooled. Fortunately for those committed to rational individualism, it is not only illegitimate, but also unnecessary, to invoke a *deus ex machina* to rescue rational individual agents from the State of Nature. They will escape by their own efforts, by rationally following rules of action whereby each individual enforces his own rights by himself punishing violators, thus deterring others from violating his rights.

Since individual agents can enforce their own rights, it is not necessary to assume the existence of the state to explain the existence of property rights. Furthermore, it is not legitimate simply to *assume* the existence of the state in a radical, general equilibrium analysis of social institutions. The bundle of various rights and duties we call the state is itself a theoretical construct or fiction we use to describe agents' behaviour when they follow rules of action. The existence of the state is as problematic as that of property rights.

This is not to deny that, at many times and places, each individual plays only a minor role in defining and enforcing his own property rights; it is only to deny that state enforcement is logically necessary for property rights to exist. We can well believe that it would be rational for two or more agents to contract for the exchange of assistance in detecting or punishing other violators of their property, or to accept third party arbitration to define property rights in the event of a disagreement. These contracts in turn, however, would ultimately have to be enforced by rules of action followed by the contracting parties themselves. The state may be thought of as a meta-institution, which helps (but is not logically essential) in enforcing institutions such as property rights. In doing so, however, the state does not *eliminate* the need for the trust and deterrence provided by the following of rules — it merely changes the focus of that need. If the first and second parties to a contract cannot, for some reason, follow rules which will ensure that each can either deter the other from violating or trust him not to do so, then they may well seek third party enforcement. But then each must trust the third party to follow a rule of enforcing the contract, or else follow a rule to deter him from failing to enforce the contract. Introducing government into my anarchistic Social Equilibrium would complicate the story, but would not fundamentally change it. Social institutions are ultimately enforced only by the rules of action rationally followed by individual agents.

Notes

1. The example is Michael Parkin's. The distinction between equilibrium and stability experiments is from Patinkin (1965).
2. Those who dismiss the State of Nature by arguing that human survival and procreation would be impossible without, at least, the family, for instance, are thus missing the point.
3. Embarrassing, that is, for those who believe both that stealing is morally wrong and that progressive income taxes are morally right. A distinction could perhaps be based on arguing that, given that some stealing will (or ought?) take place in equilibrium, it is more efficient that stealing be a government monopoly. Proper consideration of such normative issues is, however, outside our present scope.
4. This is argued in Hayek (1942).

5

Functionalism and the Limits of Trust

5.1 The Question

The Functionalist approach to the study of social institutions explains the existence of social institutions by the functions they perform. The particular function on which Functionalist economists focus attention is that of efficiency, or Pareto Optimality. Thus according to this approach, those institutions which exist are those which are most efficient in the given circumstances.

As I argued in Chapter 2, the Functionalist Approach is logically inadequate as an explanation of the existence of social institutions. The function of an institution is part of the *consequences* of the existence of that institution, and such *consequences* do not *ipso facto* explain the *causes* of the existence of an institution. The fact that an efficient allocation of resources would occur, if everyone were to obey the rules of a given social institution, does not entail that it would be rational for each individual to choose to act in conformity to those rules. For example, it might be best if nobody dropped litter, but unless the rule against dropping litter is effectively enforced by appropriate penalties, each individual agent will find it in his self-interest to disregard the rule.

But even though we reject the idea that to demonstrate the efficiency of an institution is *ipso facto* to explain the existence of that institution, it is nevertheless interesting to ask whether or not social institutions are, in fact, efficient. In particular, if social institutions are none other than the rules of action followed by rational individual agents, as I have argued, will the institutions that result turn out to be efficient? Can we resurrect Functionalism on an 'as if' basis? Will the outcome of agents' rule following behaviour be the same as if agents' behaviour were constrained by an efficient set of exogenously imposed institutional constraints?

If the answer to this question is affirmative, then it could be argued that, rather than overthrowing Functionalism, what I have done instead is to have provided a microtheoretic foundation for Functionalism by deriving Functionalist predictions from rational individual behaviour. If not, then Functionalism, even as an 'as if' theory, must be discarded.

5.2   The Meaning of Efficiency

Like most economists, I use the word 'efficiency' as shorthand for 'Pareto Optimality'. An allocation is said to be Pareto Optimal if it is not possible to make one agent better off without making some other agent worse off.

This definition of efficiency appears to be quite precise, but this appearance is deceptive. The particular source of imprecision that concerns us here is that which arises from the word 'possible'. 'Possible' always means 'possible without violating a (specified) set of constraints', and the set of constraints specified therefore determines what one means by saying that an allocation is, or is not, efficient. In order to make the concept of efficiency *precise* one must specify what those constraints are. In order to make the concept *interesting* one must specify a set of constraints which is neither too loose, nor too restrictive.

The dangers of defining too loose a set of constraints are well known. Taking an extreme case, if one defined the constraints as being merely the rules of logic, so that an allocation is efficient only if it is not *logically possible* to find an allocation in which all are better off, then the observation that existing allocations are inefficient in this sense is perfectly correct, but also perfectly irrelevant.

To avoid this obvious danger from specifying too loose a set of constraints, we may tighten the set of constraints to make due allowance for the things that limit what is *practically* feasible for us to achieve — the laws of physics at least, the niggardliness of nature, human preferences and technological knowledge as well, and perhaps human selfishness, ignorance, and even stupidity should be counted among the things that limit what is possible in practice. But in running away from the obvious dangers of specifying the constraints too loosely, we may run into the less obvious danger which arises from specifying the constraints too tightly. If we specify as constraints *all* those things which collectively determine which allocation in fact exists, then it is a trivial tautology to say that the allocation which exists is efficient given those constraints, for the very simple reason that, by assumption, *no* other allocation, whether happier or less happy, is possible given those constraints. If an economist logically deduces that a certain equilibrium outcome will result from a certain set of assumptions about preferences, technology, etc. then, if the set of constraints specified in defining efficiency is identical to the set of assumptions used to derive his results, it follows purely as a matter of logic that his equilibrium outcome will be efficient. For an outcome to be inefficient requires that another outcome be possible, and what the economist claims to have demonstrated in deriving his results is that no other outcome is logically compatible with his assumptions.

The truth of the statement that all outcomes are efficient, subject to the constraint of the assumptions which entail those outcomes, is quite independent of whether or not that outcome is, in some sense, an 'equilibrium', and is quite independent of whether or not, in some sense, 'rational agents will exploit all mutually advantageous exchanges'. It simply follows from the tautology that if only one thing is possible it must be the best thing possible (and is also, of course, the worst thing possible). Only if a theory permitted more than one possible outcome given the assumptions (a model with multiple equilibria) would it be meaningful to ask whether any particular one of those possible outcomes were efficient subject to those assumptions. And even in this case, all that is worthwhile is to attempt a Pareto ranking among possible outcomes. Furthermore, such a theory could not tell us whether the allocation that in fact exists is efficient in this sense, for it fails to tell us which of the several possible outcomes in fact exists.

A useful concept of efficiency must specify a set of constraints that is neither so loose that all allocations are trivially inefficient, nor so tight that all allocations are trivially efficient.

5.3   Efficiency and Enforcement Costs

Let us consider an application of the concept of efficiency which, in my opinion, is useful and informative.

The First Theorem of Welfare Economics tells us that if a competitive equilibrium exists, then (given certain conditions concerning the completeness of markets) that equilibrium allocation is efficient. What does this mean?

In general equilibrium theory, the allocation of resources, which is the outcome of agents' interaction, is shown to be determined by the assumed values of certain parameters that are treated as exogenous to the theory. We can divide these assumptions into four distinct sets. Firstly there are agents' preferences over goods. Secondly there is the technology which describes the agents' abilities to produce goods given the resources available. Thirdly there is the amount of resources available for agents' use. Fourthly and finally, there is a set of assumptions about what we might call the institutional framework. These assumptions specify which agents own what resources (the distribution of endowments) and require agents to consume only those goods with which they are endowed or else acquire through costless exchange at prices they treat as parametric. Given these assumptions about preferences, technology, resources, and the institutional framework, the theorist can (at least in principle) predict what the resulting allocation will be.

The First Theorem of Welfare Economics tells us that any such allocation will be efficient. What is meant by this is that it is not possible to make any agent better off without making another worse off, given only the assumptions about preferences, technology and resources. The constraint of the institutional framework, which is imposed to predict the equilibrium allocation, is not imposed in the definition of efficiency. The set of constraints subject to which the outcome is efficient is a proper subset of the set of assumptions needed to predict that outcome, and so the efficiency of that outcome is not a trivial property. What the Theorem then tells us, *inter alia*, is that there exists no alternative institutional framework to that of competitive markets and private property rights, in such cases, which could lead to an allocation in which all agents are better off, given the assumed preferences, technology and resources. It also tells us that an allocation chosen by an omniscient dictator, or by altruistic agents, given those same preferences, technology and resources, could not be Pareto Superior.

Let us now consider an example where the First Theorem of Welfare Economics does not apply. Suppose that for some reason it is impossible to monitor agents' consumption of apples, so that private property rights and hence a market in apples cannot exist. It is possible, in other words, for agents to steal and consume undetected the apples produced by another agent. The result is that fewer apples will be produced than if a market in apples did exist, since apple producers would receive only a fraction of the fruit of their labour and so would shift resources into other areas instead.

In exactly the same sense in which a competitive equilibrium with complete markets will be efficient, so a competitive equilibrium with incomplete markets will be (generally) inefficient. It will generally be possible to find an allocation of resources, subject to the same constraints on preferences, technology and resources, which makes all agents better off than the allocation that results under the institutional framework of private property and competitive markets for all goods except apples. The reason is simply that an agent who produces more apples than it would be rational for him to produce creates an external benefit to those who steal his apples which may exceed his additional costs. When markets are complete, an omniscient dictator, or an outbreak of altruism, cannot lead to a superior allocation. When markets are incomplete they could. An omniscient dictator (which here means one who knows everything that is known by any individual agent) could simply order agents to produce more apples. An outbreak of altruism might lead each agent to produce more apples for the sake of his fellows, regardless of his own self-interest.

Now obviously, unless importing a benevolent and omniscient dictator, or else creating an outbreak of altruism, are genuine policy options, the observation that allocations under incomplete markets are inefficient in the above sense carries no policy implications whatsoever in itself. 'Market failure' in this sense does not mean that we ought to attempt to create non-market institutions. Such attempts might fail to produce the desired institutions and, even if successful, those institutions in practice might perform even worse than the markets they replace. Our concern here, however, is not with discovering what policies we *ought* to follow. We are concerned with what sorts of institutions will *in fact* exist.

Now, in constructing the above example I provided a reason for the non-existence of private property rights and markets in apples — I assumed that it was impossible for agents to monitor another agent's consumption of apples, so that each agent can steal and consume apples with no risk of detection. Any reader who accepts this assumption as explaining why the social institutions of private property rights and markets in apples will not exist, *ipso facto* rejects Functionalism. My assumption does not *logically* entail the non-existence of those institutions. Indeed, if Functionalism were correct, my assumption would provide no reason at all for supposing those institutions not to exist. My assumption does, however, provide an explanation of why those institutions do not exist, if we accept the theory of social institutions that I have put forward here.

The Functionalist theory of social institutions views social institutions as a set of institutional constraints on agents' behaviour analogous to the constraints imposed on their behaviour by the physical environment. Individual agents choose their actions rationally, subject to both institutional and natural constraints. The Functionalist thesis asserts that of all the possible sets of institutional constraints, that set which results in the most efficient outcome, given agents' preferences, information and natural environment, is that which will exist.

Suppose Functionalism were correct. There is nothing to prevent each agent from acting as if he were constrained not to pick and consume the apples grown by another agent. Each agent would know himself whether his actions did or did not violate this constraint, even if, by assumption, other agents cannot know this. If all agents were to abide by this constraint, then all could be better off than if they failed to do so. Barring other 'market failures', the allocation of resources that would result if agents acted thus — respecting an imaginary taboo against stealing apples — would be efficient subject to preferences, technology and resources. Thus if Functionalism were true, property rights and hence markets in apples would be predicted to exist despite the assumed inability of agents to monitor the stealing of apples by others. The fact that this prediction is false — that where theft cannot be monitored theft is common — is exactly what we would predict from the assumption of rational *individual* behaviour and therefore demonstrates the falsity of Functionalism. Self-seeking rational individuals do not always respect constraints that it would be in the interests of each for *all* to respect. They only respect those constraints that are in the interests of each individual to respect.

A defender of Functionalism may reply that I have prejudiced the case against his thesis by requiring too strict a definition of efficiency, and thus destroying only a straw man. If for some reason it is impossible to monitor the stealing of apples, then it is unreasonable to expect an allocation of resources as efficient as could be attained if it were possible to monitor the thefts. Functionalism says that social institutions are efficient. The definition of Functionalism depends on the definition of efficiency. Any reasonable definition of efficiency would take into account the costs of enforcing institutional constraints. If it is impossible to monitor theft of apples then it is impossible to enforce property rights in apples, which means that the costs of enforcing the institutional constraint in this case are infinite. Once these costs are taken into account, he argues, it is no longer efficient to have property rights in apples, and so Functionalism predicts that they will not exist.

This argument sounds reasonable. It is far too reasonable. What it does is to convert Functionalism from an interesting, if false, theory about social institutions into a vacuous tautology.

To see that Functionalism becomes a vacuous tautology if we define efficiency to include actual costs of enforcing institutions, let us first note that if the costs of enforcing different possible institutions were left unspecified, or theoretically indeterminate, then Functionalism would obviously be vacuous. If we can say nothing about the costs of enforcing alternative institutions, then *any* of those alternative institutions could be the most efficient, taking those unspecified costs into account. In order to escape the charge of vacuity in this direction then, the Functionalist must be prepared, at least in principle, to specify some or other theory that could predict the costs of enforcing each of the possible alternative institutions. Now the costs of enforcing an institution depend on the behaviour of individuals — both of those who would enforce the constraints and of those who are to obey the constraints (who may, of course, be the same people). For example, the costs of enforcing the institution of property rights depends, let us say, on the number of policemen needed to keep the amount of theft to some level deemed tolerable. The number of policemen needed would be higher if each individual policeman were less willing to apprehend and prosecute thieves, and if individual thieves were more willing to risk being caught. In order to know the costs of enforcing a set of institutional constraints on agents' behaviour, we therefore need a theory of agents' behaviour in enforcing and obeying those constraints. But, if we have such a theory, we *ipso facto* have a theory that can predict, at least in principle, *which* institutional constraints agents will in fact enforce and obey. In order to specify the costs of enforcing alternative institutions, and so rescue Functionalism from one charge of vacuity, we need a theory of those costs. This theory, it turns out, would in itself tell us which of those alternative institutions will in fact exist, and so make Funtionalism itself redundant.

To recap the above argument: Functionalism asserts that it is the most efficient of the many possible alternative institutions which will in fact exist. If the concept of efficiency thereby invoked ignores the costs of enforcing institutions, Functionalism is obviously false. To escape being obviously false it must define efficiency to include the costs of enforcing the alternative institutional constraints, but in doing so it is faced with a dilemma: it either does not specify what determines those costs, and so is vacuous, or else it does specify the determinants of those costs, and in doing so constrains the concept of efficiency so tightly that only one of the alternative institutions can possibly be enforced and obeyed — in which case that one institution is vacuously the most (and least) efficient of all possible institutions, for there is only one that is possible.

5.4 The Source of Inefficiency

From now on we shall define efficiency in the same way as that concept is used in the First Theorem of Welfare Economics — an allocation is efficient if it is not possible to make one agent better off and no agent worse off subject to the constraints of preferences, technology and resources. More precisely, an allocation is efficient if, and only if, it is not possible to specify additional constraints on agents' behaviour, regardless of whether individual agents would wish to violate those constraints, that could result in a Pareto Superior allocation. For example, an allocation is not efficient in our sense if adding a taboo against dropping litter could make all agents better off.

This definition of efficiency is an interesting and useful one to apply in contexts where we wish to examine the extent to which social institutions lead to efficient outcomes. It is constrained neither too loosely so that efficiency is always unattainable, nor too tightly so that efficiency is always and trivially attained. Social institutions will sometimes be efficient in this sense, and sometimes inefficient.

The question we now seek to address is this: if what constitutes the set of social institutions is none other than the rules of action which rational individual agents choose to follow and are believed to follow, then in what circumstances will those institutions be efficient or inefficient? When will rational rule-following individual behaviour lead to efficient outcomes?

The general prima-facie case for expecting outcomes to be efficient is provided by the 'Coase theorem'.[1] Suppose that an allocation of resources were not efficient. This would entail that a further reallocation of resources — additional exchanges of goods — could make all agents better off (or no worse off). But why should rational agents ever fail to agree to such exchanges which could make each better off? How is it logically possible that a rational agent could ever fail to act in his own (perceived) best interest? If we accept these last two questions as rhetorical then we accept that the initial inefficient allocation can be hypothetical only — an assumption made in order to derive a contradiction and so demonstrate the truth of its negation — and that if all agents are rational the only allocations that can in fact exist are efficient allocations. I do not, however, accept these questions as rhetorical.

The well-known game of Prisoner's Dilemma illustrates the possibility that rational agents may fail to take actions which would result in a mutually beneficial reallocation of resources. Taking the other player's choice as given, regardless of what that choice is, each player is better off if he chooses the 'non-co-operative' action. The Nash equilibrium applies, therefore, where both choose the 'non-co-operative' action, even though both would be better off if both were to choose the 'co-operative' action. The outcome is thus that the rational players choose a non-Pareto Optimal, or inefficient, allocation of resources.

Why is it that the 'Coase theorem' fails in the case of Prisoner's Dilemma? The answer is that the players in Prisoner's Dilemma are unable to enforce exchanges. Suppose that one player were able to commit himself conspicuously to a contingent strategy. Were he able to do this, he would commit himself to adopt the 'co-operative' action if, and only if, the other player chose the 'co-operative' action. Faced with this commitment, the second player must choose between the jointly 'co-operative' and the jointly 'non-co-operative' outcomes. He will rationally choose the former. In making this commitment the first player is, in effect, offering the second player an exchange: 'I will give you something that you value (choosing the 'co-operative' action) if, and only if, you give me something that I value'.

The game of Prisoner's Dilemma results in an inefficient outcome because the players are unable to enforce exchanges — they are unable to make credible commitments. If both players move simultaneously, so that each makes his choice of action in ignorance of the other's choice, then it is obvious that neither can commit to a contingent strategy. Neither can make his choice contingent on the other's choice because he must choose before observing the other's choice. Now suppose instead that they choose in turn, so that the second player observes the first player's move before he makes his move. Suppose the second player promises to 'co-operate' if, and only if, the first player 'co-operates'. Suppose the first player believes this promise, and so 'co-operates'. Would the second player actually carry out his promise, and 'co-operate' too? In a single game he would not rationally do so. Since the first player's move has now been taken, it is part of history and cannot be influenced by what happens afterwards. Taking the first player's choice as given, the second player will rationally choose not to 'co-operate'. Once the behaviour he has sought to elicit by making his promise has been performed, it is no longer rational for the second player to perform his promised action. Here again is the problem of the time-inconsistency of optimal plans. Being able to predict that the second player will rationally break his promise, the first player would never have believed that promise in the first place, and so would also have chosen the 'non-co-operative' move. Thus even when the two players move sequentially, the outcome of Prisoner's Dilemma is still inefficient.

The reason why the 'Coase theorem' fails — the reason why rational agents sometimes fail to make mutually beneficial exchanges — is then simply that exchanges cannot always be enforced. An exchange is always a contingent commitment, in which one agent precommits his future actions contingent upon another agent's action — he commits to giving if, and only if, the other gives. The failures of rational agents to achieve efficient outcomes are thus ultimately failures of commitment — the inability of agents to communicate credible contingent promises. Failures of efficiency result from: firstly, inability to *communicate* promises; secondly, inability to communicate *credible* promises; and thirdly, inability to communicate credible *contingent* promises. These are the three sources of inefficiency.

5.5 The Limits of Trust

On the first source of inefficiency — the inability to *communicate* promises — I have little to say. It is obvious that agents may have difficulty in making a mutually beneficial exchange, for instance, if they lack a common language in which to negotiate the terms of trade and to express commitments. If the agents never meet at all it may be harder still. But although difficult, exchange need not be impossible in such circumstances. The role of language is simply to make it easier to learn what it is that the other side wants and is prepared to give up to get it. It may be possible to learn these things simply from the context (observing a man in the desert with no water, but lots of food) or simply by trial and error. If each can somehow learn the other's preferences, he can learn the commitment that it *would be rational* for the other to make, even if he lacks a language with which he can *express* that commitment, and, provided trust is present, the former alone is sufficient. When trust is not present, the mere *expression* of commitment means nothing. Lack of a common language may certainly have hindered mutually advantageous exchange between settlers and natives, but it certainly did not always prevent it.

Let us suppose that there are no problems of communication. Let us also postpone consideration of the second source of inefficiency, that of the credibility of promises. We will assume that all promises are accepted with complete confidence, meaning by this that everyone expects the promisor to fulfil his promise, regardless of whether he would *wish* to do so, provided only that he is *able* to do so.

Consider once again the game of Prisoner's Dilemma. Let us now suppose, however, that the two players are able to meet beforehand and can communicate credible promises. Does this always enable the players to attain the efficient outcome, where both co-operate?

If the moves are made sequentially, so that the second player observes the first player's move before making his move, then all that is required is that the second player be able to communicate credible promises. The second player will promise to choose the 'co-operative' action if, and only if, the first player also chooses the 'co-operative' action. By assumption, the first player will believe in this promise, and will rationally choose to 'co-operate', and the second player will then carry out his promise and the outcome will be efficient.

Now suppose that the moves are made simultaneously, so that neither observes the other's move when making his move. In the simultaneous game, it is no longer enough that only one player can communicate credible promises. A promise cannot be made contingent on the other player's move because the promisor will not have *observed* that move, and so will be *unable* to carry out such a contingent promise. *Unilateral* trust is not enough to attain efficiency in the simultaneous game; *bilateral* trust is needed. Only if *both* players can make credible promises will the efficient outcome be attainable. With bilateral trust, one player can promise to choose the 'co-operative' action if, and only if, the second player *promises* to choose the 'co-operative' action. The promise is made contingent on the other's *promising* to play 'co-operatively', which *can* be observed, rather than on his *actually* playing 'co-operatively', which *cannot* be observed. But such a contingent promise would rationally be made only if the promise on which it was contingent was credible; thus *bilateral* trust is required.

An example of the need for bilateral trust is provided by what is called the 'principal–agent problem'.[2] The principal's utility is indirectly affected by the agent's action, which the principal cannot observe. The problem faced by the principal is to find some incentive scheme to induce the agent to act in the principal's interest. For instance, the owner of a company wants his manager to maximize the company's profits, which depend on the manager's effort and on general market conditions, neither of which the owner can observe. If the owner pays the manager a fixed salary and keeps the residual profit then the manager has no incentive to work hard. If on the other hand the owner pays himself a fixed salary and leaves the residual profit to the manager, the manager has a sufficient incentive to work hard, but has to bear all the risk from market fluctuations. In the absence of trust, the best that can be attained is some sort of unhappy compromise between these two extremes. With perfect trust the problem disappears. The manager simply promises to work hard in exchange for a promise of a fixed salary.

Another example of the need for bilateral trust is provided by the 'market for lemons'.[3] Suppose that the buyer of a good (for instance a used car) does not know the quality of that good, but that the seller does. The buyer cannot promise to pay a price contingent on the quality of the good he is sold because he cannot observe that quality. Sellers thus receive the same price for good and bad cars, and so tend to sell only the bad cars, while keeping the good ones for themselves. The result is that the market for good used cars tends to dry up. Again, with perfect trust the problem disappears. The buyer simply promises to pay a price which is contingent on the quality of the car that the seller promises to sell. The buyer can observe the *promised* quality, even if he cannot observe the *actual* quality.

Provided agents can communicate promises, perfect multilateral trust would eliminate the problems of enforcing exchanges. If all exchanges could be enforced, rational agents would never permit an inefficient allocation of resources to exist. Functionalism — the view that existing institutions are always efficient — is thus seen to presuppose perfect trust between all agents — to assume that all agents believe that any promise that can be fulfilled will be fulfilled. This assumption is obviously false. The predictions of Functionalism are false because trust is not always perfect.

5.6   Imperfect Reputations

In Chapter 2, when describing what it means for an agent to follow a rule, I said that an agent who follows a rule acts as if he had precommitted his future actions. There is, however, this important difference between following a rule and precommitment: the only incentive an agent can have for continuing to act in accordance with his rule is that contrary actions might lead to the loss of his reputation for following that rule. Since the value of this reputation will generally be finite, an agent's benefits from acting expediently may, under some circumstances, exceed his expected costs from the risk of losing his reputation. In such circumstances a rational agent would choose to act expediently. Furthermore, if other agents are aware of his costs and benefits, they will expect him to act expediently and depart from his rule under such circumstances. Thus, following a rule is like precommitment except that there is a limit to what one can credibly precommit. In some cases this limit will be binding, and rational rule-individualists will behave quite differently from agents who could conspicuously attach guns to their own heads which would fire automatically if they broke their commitments.

The value of an agent's reputation for following a rule is the difference between his utility if he continues and is expected to continue to follow that rule, and his utility if he acts and is expected to act in a purely discretionary manner. In deciding whether or not to depart from his rule, a rational agent will weigh the benefits of departure against the expected costs — these being the value of his reputation multiplied by the probability that his departure will be observed and his reputation lost.

One obvious reason then for reputation being insufficient to enforce commitments is if other agents cannot observe whether an agent has departed from his rule or not. In the example of the principal–agent problem above, for instance, the manager would violate his promise to work hard, because he knows that the owner cannot observe how hard he is working. And knowing the manager would rationally violate his promise, the owner would never believe that promise.

Another reason for reputation being insufficient to enforce commitments is if there are no long-term relationships between agents. When a used car is exchanged, for instance, it is often unlikely that buyer and seller will ever do business together again. If so, the value of the seller's reputation in the eyes of that buyer is zero. Even if the buyer discovers that, contrary to the seller's promise, the car he has just bought is a 'lemon', the seller loses nothing when he loses the trust of that particular buyer. On the other hand, if the seller is in the business of selling used cars, and the news spreads by word of mouth, he may value his reputation more highly. Yet even so, the loss of repeat business from the buyer and his friends may be insufficient to match the benefits of selling a lemon at the price of a good quality car.

The labour market presents additional examples to show that reputation can sometimes fail to be sufficient to enforce all mutually advantageous exchanges. Employment nearly always presents opportunities for the worker to 'cheat' his employer, by shirking or stealing for example. If cheating benefits the worker less than it costs the employer, then both could gain if the worker were prevented from cheating and received higher wages in compensation, but can this exchange be enforced?

Suppose the labour market functioned according to the simple textbook model, with wages adjusting to equate the supply and demand of anonymous workers. If the only penalty an employer could inflict on a worker caught cheating is to fire him, that penalty would be no penalty at all, for the worker could immediately get another job at exactly the same wage, and so loses nothing. Faced with this problem, an employer might decide to pay higher than market wages. Now if a worker is caught cheating and is fired he will suffer a reduction in wages, and so might be deterred from cheating. If the costs of cheating are high for the employer relative to the benefits for the worker, it might pay the employer to raise wages sufficiently to deter cheating.

Now, if it pays one employer to raise wages above the market level in order to deter cheating, it may pay all employers to do likewise. It is not possible, of course, for all employers to pay wages higher than the market level, but the attempt by each to do so causes the market level of wages to rise. As wages rise the demand for labour falls and creates an excess supply of labour — unemployment. With higher unemployment it will take longer for a fired worker to get a new job, and the loss of wages in the interim is the penalty of being fired. In equilibrium the level of unemployment will be just sufficient to deter cheating and so individual employers will not need to raise wages further.[4]

What causes unemployment in this example is the inability of unemployed workers credibly to promise not to 'cheat' an employer who hires them. If workers caught 'cheating' could be fined, or else be given bad references which could damage their reputations in the eyes of future employers, unemployment could be reduced or possibly even eliminated, for fines or loss of reputation might constitute penalties sufficient to deter cheating and thus eliminate the need for high wages and the resulting unemployment as a penalty. Unfortunately, using fines or letters of reference may solve the problem of the employer's trusting the worker, but it creates in its place a problem of the worker's trusting his employer. If only the worker, and occasionally his employer, can monitor whether or not the worker is cheating, what is to prevent the employer from blackmailing a worker by threatening to make false accusations of cheating and so forcing the worker to incur a fine or damage his reputation? In any exchange, each side gives up something he values in order to induce the other to give up something that the other values. Whoever is the first to receive the other's goods always has an incentive to keep those goods without giving up any of his goods in return. Whoever is the first to give up his goods must therefore trust the recipient to carry out his promise of making payment. Changing the order of play does not eliminate the need for trust, it merely changes the focus of that trust from one player to the other.

5.7 Conclusion

Exchange requires trust. Trust must be based upon agents having reputations sufficiently valuable that they would not rationally risk losing their reputations by violating that trust. Even when exchanges are enforced by third parties, as when the partners sign a legally binding written contract, this does not eliminate the need for trust; it merely shifts the focus of trust on to those third parties, who in turn will take pains to enforce the contract between first and second parties fairly only if they value their reputations more than the bribes that first or second parties could offer.

Sometimes the value of their reputations will be sufficient to enable agents to undertake mutually advantageous and hence efficiency promoting exchanges. In such cases agents' exchanges will indeed be as if the institutional framework within which exchange takes place were the efficient, exogenously imposed structure imagined by Functionalism. At other times, because of imperfect communication, imperfect monitoring or few opportunities for repeated exchanges, the value of reputation will be insufficient to enforce exchanges. In such cases, mutually advantageous exchanges will not be made. Furthermore, since the value of an agent's reputation depends on the value to him of future exchanges, which in turn depends on the price he will receive in those future exchanges (as when the worker's decision not to cheat depends on the wage he expects to be paid), the price at which exchanges take place will depend not merely upon supply and demand but also on the need for agents to provide each other with sufficient incentives not to break their exchange commitments. The institutional framework within which exchange takes place (the rule of keeping promises) is not independent of the actions which take place within that framework (the prices and quantities of goods exchanged). Knowing this, rational agents will modify their behaviour within that framework in order to preserve the existence of that very same framework. This is why the predictions of Functionalism fail. Human action is not always as it would be if it took place within an efficient, exogenously imposed set of institutional constraints.

Notes

1. See Coase (1960).
2. For a survey of the principal–agent problem, see for example Macdonald (1984).
3. The term is taken from the title of Akerlof (1979).
4. The idea that enforcement problems can cause wage differentials and/or unemployment, has been modelled by, for example, Calvo and Wellisz (1979), Gintis and Bowles (1981), and Shapiro and Stiglitz (1984). Its origin can perhaps be traced to Adam Smith's (1776) *Wealth of Nations*.

   It is most important, however, to distinguish two versions of the thesis. The 'conspiracy theory' version has it that employers *choose* to create unemployment in order to discipline workers, so that the *function* of unemployment is to prevent workers from striking. This version is inadmissible from an individualist perspective, since no single employer is able to create unemployment (unless of course he is a monopsonist). The second version has it that unemployment is an *unintended consequence* of the attempts by individual employers to discipline workers by raising relative wages. The attempt by each employer to raise relative wages must, by the laws of mathematics, fail in aggregate, but creates unemployment as a by-product. And, contrary to the functionalist thesis, there is no presumption whatsoever that the amount of unemployment created is optimal from either the employers' or society's point of view.

6

Conflict and Consensus

6.1 Introduction

A conflict is a struggle over the distribution of rights. The two (or more) parties to the conflict each claim rights such that the two claims are incompatible. The conflict ends when one, or both sides, makes sufficient concessions in terms of the rights it is able or willing to defend that the two claims become compatible. In the time it takes for the conflict to be thus resolved, however, the struggle over the distribution of rights has imposed costs on the parties involved.

Strikes (and lock-outs) are one such example of costly conflict. What is in dispute is the division of the joint rents to the trading relationship between employer and worker. The employer refuses to accept a level of wages (or other benefits or conditions of work) which would be acceptable to the worker, who in turn refuses to accept a level of wages which would be acceptable to the employer. Strikes are costly. The very conflict over the distribution of the joint rents to their trading relationship destroys some portion of those rents, for the conflict takes the form of a suspension of that trading relationship.

Wars are another example of costly conflict. A typical war between nations may be a struggle over the right of sovereignty to a particular area of land — over where the boundary between the two nations is to lie. Once again, the struggle imposes costs on the parties involved, but in a different form — resources needed to produce weapons, destroyed capital equipment, the labour of the soldiers, and the loss of lives and limbs.

Even those conflicts that are resolved by the courts are not without apparently avoidable costs. The parties to a civil dispute can reduce or eliminate lawyers' fees and other court costs if they negotiate an out of court settlement.

In all these conflicts there exists a pie which must somehow be divided between the two parties. If the division of the pie is determined by conflict, the total size of the pie is reduced by the amount of the total costs of that conflict. It is this fact which makes the occurrence of costly conflict such a puzzling phenomenon. For in any division of the smaller post-conflict pie, and any division of the larger pre-conflict pie, at least one and perhaps both parties will get more pie under the pre-conflict division. Furthermore, for any division of the post-conflict pie there exists at least one possible division of the pre-conflict pie such that both parties will get more under that latter division. Faced with a choice between conflict and accepting that pre-conflict division, each side would rationally reject conflict. Why then do presumably rational agents, in choosing conflict, fail to act in their own best interests? In other words, an allocation of resources achieved through conflict is not Pareto Optimal. With no conflict there always exists a Pareto Superior allocation. Why then do presumably rational agents, in choosing a non-Pareto Optimal allocation, fail to undertake a mutually beneficial exchange in which each concedes some of his claimed rights in return for a similar concession from the other, and so negotiate a settlement without resort to conflict?

The existence of costly conflict thus seems to present a paradox or anomaly to those who view social interaction as the outcome of rational behaviour by self-interested individuals, for in choosing conflict individuals appear to act against their rational self-interest. My own solution to this paradox is to consider not the rationality of the *actions* of the individuals involved in conflict, but the rationality of their *rules of action*. In order to have rights, an agent must follow a rule of action whereby he imposes costs on those who transgress his rights — costs of sufficient magnitude to deter transgressions. If the set of rights thereby created and enforced by several individual agents are mutually compatible, then no conflicts occur. The presence of uncertainty, however, can create incompatibility. Imperfect knowledge of the location of the boundary between two agents' rights creates the possibility of an overlap between their respective claims. In that case, by exercising what he perceives as his rights each is perceived as transgressing the rights of the other, who is then required by his rule of action to punish that transgression. Should he be seen to fail to follow his rule of punishing transgressions, an agent would lose his reputation for doing so, would fail to deter future transgressions, and would thus lose his ability to enforce his rights. Conflicts are thus exercises in mutual punishment, each playing policeman to the other's thief. Only by imposing mutual costs at least equal in value to the disputed rights — in effect destroying the disputed property — can agents preserve the existence of rights at all. Given uncertainty, the occasional occurrence of costly conflict over the distribution of rights is a prerequisite for there being any rights to distribute.

6.2   The Hicksian Theory

The existence of costly conflict poses a problem for those who follow the economic approach for it appears as if rational agents, in failing to negotiate a settlement without resort to costly conflict, fail to make a mutually advantageous exchange and thus fail to act in their own best interests. I have stated my own answer to this problem, but before exploring that answer, we will first examine the existing economic theory of conflict, which I shall call the Hicksian theory.

Acccording to the theory presented in Hicks (1964), conflicts occur because the parties have different expectations of the outcome. Suppose each side expects, for instance, that the post-conflict division would yield it the whole of the remaining pie, with the other side getting none. Even if both sides know that the costs of conflict will reduce the size of the total pie by one third, there exists no pre-conflict division such that both sides *expect* to do better by accepting that division than by resorting to conflict. In such a case each would require more than two-thirds of the original pie to persuade it to renounce conflict. Thus, according to the Hicksian theory, even though an allocation of resources achieved through costly conflict cannot be *actually* Pareto Optimal, it may be *perceived* by the parties as Pareto Optimal, in the sense that no other allocation is *expected* by both sides to be better. Since people act in accordance to what they *perceive* as their self-interest, which is not always the same as their actual self-interest, the puzzle of apparently irrational behaviour in conflict is resolved.

The puzzle is not really resolved by this theory, however, it is merely postponed. Given their jointly over-optimistic beliefs, their actions in choosing conflict may indeed be rational, but could it ever be rational for the parties to hold these jointly over-optimistic beliefs?

There is no difficulty in allowing that an expectation of the outcome of conflict, based on incomplete information, may turn out to have been mistakenly optimistic after the event. There is also no difficulty in allowing that both parties' expectations may be mistakenly optimistic, if those expectations are formed in isolation, so that neither side knows what the other expects. The difficulty is that in rejecting a negotiated settlement and choosing conflict, each side *ipso facto* reveals its expectations to the other. At the very moment that conflict starts, each side knows that there exists this divergence of expectations which has caused the conflict. A rational agent, on learning that another rational agent with partially independent information has a different expectation than he has, should immediately revise his expectation towards that of the other. If the Hicksian theory were correct, the existence of conflict would make it common knowledge between both sides that their expectations diverged, and, if agents form their expectations rationally, such a situation should persist for no longer than it took agents to realize that the divergence existed. Thus if conflicts ever did *start* as predicted by the Hicksian theory, they should almost immediately *stop*, whereas actual conflicts, and hence the divergence of expectations which is alleged to cause them, may persist for days, weeks, months, or even years. The Hicksian theory, at best, gives no explanation of the *duration* of conflicts. Those versions of the Hicksian theory, such as Cross (1965), which do seem to yield predictions about the duration of conflict, only get those predictions by assuming a slow and non-rational process of expectations revision.[1]

The duration of conflicts is surely one of their key aspects, which a satisfactory theory of conflict should be able to explain. That the Hicksian theory provides no explanation of duration (whereas my own theory does) is therefore a major failing of that theory. There is, however, a second failure of the Hicksian theory which is of even greater importance.

The Hicksian theory interprets conflict as wholly anomic — as an exercise in naked bargaining power unaffected by any normative considerations. It considers each side as trying to get as much as it is *able* to get, by whatever method is most causally effective, regardless of what it thinks it is *entitled* to get, or *ought* to get, and regardless of what methods it thinks are *legitimate*. Now some may not see this as a failure of the theory, or may even see it as a virtue, but it is a failure for the following three reasons.

The first reason why an anomic theory of conflict is unsatisfactory is that it can make no sense of the heavily normative content of what the parties to the conflict describe themselves as doing — it can make no sense of their moralistic propaganda, if you like. A party to a conflict very rarely confesses that it is engaged in conflict simply because it thinks it can gain more by conflict than by negotiation, which is what the Hicksian theory claims its reason is. Instead, it will usually claim that its cause is, in some sense, just, that it deserves to get what it demands, that it is defending its rights, and that it is in the right and the other side is in the wrong. Now a Hicksian theorist could, of course, reply that these pronouncements are not to be taken seriously — that they result from either self-deception or the cynical attempt to deceive others, and are merely a façade which has no effect on actual behaviour. But if conflicts were in fact purely exercises in bargaining power, and normative pronouncements irrelevant to the actual behaviour of either side, why would the parties expend the resources they do in making and publicizing those pronouncements? Why would propagandists consistently believe that their audience can be fooled? At the very least, the fact that propaganda exists means that the propagandist believes it to be effective, but then if he thinks it effective, his success in winning the propaganda war will affect his willingness to continue the actual war and thus will, in fact, be effective in determining the actual outcome. The expectation of the effectiveness of propaganda must be somehow self-fulfilling, for propaganda has passed the test of the market. Rational agents will not indefinitely continue to pay for a totally useless good. The normative content of pronouncements during a conflict cannot be a façade unless expectations are irrational.

The second reason why an anomic theory of conflict is unsatisfactory is that it fails to explain why conflicts are nearly always to some extent 'contained' – in that both sides nearly always forego the use of some apparently effective weapons. In the case of the Hicksian theory applied to strikes, for example, workers withdraw their labour because their doing so imposes costs on the employer and makes him willing to concede higher wages in order to avoid those costs. Yet there are many other ways that workers could impose costs on their employer, which could impose higher costs on the employer at less cost to themselves. Why are arson and personal violence not more frequently and generally used in industrial disputes? Similarly, why did Britain and the United States fail to use nuclear weapons in the Falkland and Vietnam wars? Why do parties to a conflict not always use the most cost-effective ways of imposing costs on the other side? Why do they use weapons which sometimes hurt them as much, or even more than, they hurt the enemy? How could doing so possibly improve one's bargaining power? The Hicksian theory cannot explain why conflicts are contained in these ways. My own theory can.

The third reason why an anomic theory of conflict is unsatisfactory is that conflicts are disputes about the distribution of *rights*, and those very rights would be meaningless were human interaction wholly anomic. The Hicksian theory fails to provide an integrated theory of human interaction which can incorporate both the fact that rights exist — that human behaviour defends, respects, and thus creates rights — and that those same rights are the objects of conflict. How could the people who created those rights be the very same people who now fight for those rights regardless of their right to do so? In contrast to the Hicksian theory of conflict, my theory sees both the existence of rights and the conflict over the distribution of rights as arising from one and the same type of human behaviour — the following of rational rules of action. It thus replaces what would have to be two quite dissimilar theories, of rights and of conflict over rights, with a single unified theory.

6.3   The Arbitrariness of the Distribution of Rights

If we were to ignore all that has happened in the past, and consider only the situation as it stands today, the existing distribution of property rights would appear quite arbitrary. There would appear to be no moral grounds, and, what is important for our concerns here, no causes to explain why this particular distribution, rather than some other distribution of property rights, is recognized by members of our society. Why should the boundary between two adjacent properties, or nations, be where it is and not several yards or miles to one side or the other? Would I still be believed to owe a certain amount of money to a certain bank if everyone were to forget that in the past I had contracted a mortgage with that bank? It is a very surprising fact, in a world of rational agents for whom bygones are supposedly forever bygones, that the deck of cards representing individuals' rights is not shuffled and redealt every night — that I awake to discover that I own exactly the same things I owned when I fell asleep (barring major social upheavals).

If the current distribution of rights were determined solely by current bargaining power, then this conservatism of the distribution of rights would not be observed. It is reasonable to assume that the power of agents, and of nations, is something which varies continuously over time. If power alone created the distribution of rights, that distribution would therefore also be changing continuously. A nation losing a warship in a gale, or suffering a minor epidemic among those fit for active service, would immediately lose a few yards of its territory to adjacent nations. This is not what happens.[2]

Understood even in the positive sense, might alone does not make rights. Might merely sets limits on what rights can be enforced and, within those wide limits, it is past rights which make current rights. Today's boundary is in the same place as it was yesterday. It is as if there were friction governing the location of boundaries between different people's rights, friction sufficient to resist a considerable imbalance in relative power, so that it takes a very large imbalance to produce what will then be a large discrete jump in the distribution of rights, much as friction between plates in the earth's crust may create occasional earthquakes interrupting long periods of stasis.

There are good reasons why rational agents would not choose to recognize and enforce a boundary between their rights which fluctuated continuously according to their relative power. One side's power can be increased by the application of resources to increase it. If the position of the boundary were determined by relative power, each side would then have an incentive to invest resources in increasing its relative power in order to shift the position of the boundary in its favour. The position of the boundary would then be determined in a Nash equilibrium in which each side invests optimally in power given the investment made by the other. In equilibrium, the cost of building (say) an extra tank would exactly equal the value of the extra land that would be obtained by the increase in relative power brought about by building that tank.

It is not efficient for the position of boundaries to be determined in this manner. If both sides made a matched reduction in the amount of resources devoted to power, so that their relative power, and hence the position of the boundary, remained unchanged, both sides would now be able to devote those freed resources to other, productive uses and be better off as a result. Fixing a boundary position which is, at the margin, independent of relative power is a way to ensure just such a mutual disarmament, for it would remove each side's incentive to invest extra resources in power.

Note that there is an exact analogy between the costs of having a boundary which depends on relative power, as explained in the preceding paragraph, and the costs of transfer and protection activity in the State of Nature, as explained in Chapter 4. The very reason why rights exist at all precludes the existence of rights based solely on might. If might alone made rights there would be no point in agents creating rights. If agents choose to follow rules which create rights, the rules they will follow will create rights the boundaries to which are relatively fixed, and which do not fluctuate continuously with relative power. What I have just done, therefore, is to explain the positive fact that might alone does not create right — why the distribution of rights between agents does not fluctuate continuously with their relative power.

Those who have read Chapter 4 critically may have noticed an apparent problem — that the Social Equilibrium to that model may not be unique. The particular Social Equilibrium I chose to consider was a symmetric one, in which each agent owns exactly those goods that he himself has produced. Though this particular Social Equilibrium, being symmetric, is simpler to analyse, there may also exist other asymmetric social equilibria which could equally be enforced by the rules of action followed by individual agents. Such asymmetric equilibria would require fixed, lump-sum payments from some agents to other agents with no quid pro quo in return. For instance, one apple-producing agent could annually transfer ten apples from another apple-producing agent who engages in no protection activity to hinder that transfer. It would be as if some agents pay 'tribute' to other agents. These asymmetric social equilibria with fixed tributes would be efficient and, more importantly, could be enforceable by the same sorts of rules of action that enforce the symmetric equilibrium. Agents could be deterred from failing to pay tribute by a rule of action in which the recipient of tribute punished them for failing to pay. The symmetric Social Equilibrium is simply a Social Equilibrium in which the amount of tribute, which can be positive or negative, is set at zero. Any level of tribute could be enforced by some rule of action, provided the recipient is able to impose costs for non-payment exceeding the costs of paying tribute.

This non-uniqueness of the Social Equilibrium should not, however, be seen as an undesirable result of the theory of property rights proposed in Chapter 4. On the contrary, it is a virtue. The actual distribution of rights is in fact arbitrary in exactly the same sense as any Social Equilibrium in that model is arbitrary, and it is a virtue of the model that it thus mirrors the world it was designed to represent. The current actual distribution of rights would be arbitrary if we ignored the distribution which prevailed yesterday, which in turn depended on that which prevailed the day before. Similarly, the non-uniqueness of the Social Equilibrium is seen as a problem only if we forget that what was conducted in Chapter 4 was a *stability experiment* — an examination of what maintains the existence of the current set of rights — and was not an *historical* account of how those rights came into being in the distant past. Which *particular* distribution of rights exists at a point in time is a question of history — an outcome of an historical process of production, exchange, settlement, and indeed fraud and theft, the origins of which are poorly documented. The topic of Chapter 4 is what now *maintains* that distribution and prevents a collapse into the State of Nature.

6.4 Defining the Boundary

The defining of rights, in the literal sense of setting limits or boundaries between the rights of several agents, is a social phenomenon. By this I mean that it is not logically possible for one agent to define his rights unilaterally. What we mean when we say that an agent has a certain right is that it is widely recognized that he has that right in the relevant society. If an agent claims a right, but that right is respected by the actions of no other agent, then he does not in fact have that right. (It must be understood that when I say here an agent has a right I mean that as a positive, not normative, statement. His claim may be just, and the decision of other members of the relevant society not to recognize his claim may be unjust by our standards, but if we seek a positive explanation of his and other members' behaviour we must say that he does not, in fact, possess the claimed right.)

It is a very surprising fact that there is virtually complete agreement between members of a society on the location of the boundaries between the rights of its individual members. Or, to put the same point another way, since rights cannot exist without widespread agreement as to who has what rights, and a society is simply a collection of individual agents for whom this widespread agreement pertains, it is a very surprising fact that rights and society exist. If the boundaries between rights are arbitrary, as I have argued in the preceding section, how is it that individual agents co-ordinate their beliefs on the location of those boundaries? What is it that nearly always ensures a perfect coincidence between where I perceive the boundary to lie and where my neighbour perceives the boundary to lie? If we understand conflicts to arise from disagreements concerning the distribution or location of boundaries between rights, as I argue we must, then what is surprising from this perspective is not that conflict exists, but that it is so rare — that we observe conflict over rights as simply a minor exception compared with a massive background of agreement without which the concept of rights, and hence of conflict over rights, could not be meaningful.

To answer this question, let us return to the model presented in Chapter 4 to explain the existence of property rights. Starting from the State of Nature, where no rights exist, I argued that an agent would rationally escape the misery of the State of Nature by following a rule of action, in which he punished other agents who directed transfer activity against the goods he had produced. By being seen and believed to follow this rule, an agent could deter others from transferring goods he had produced, and so make himself better off by enabling him to switch his time away from transfer and protection into production activity, thus producing and consuming more goods. To be more specific, A would follow a 'tit-for-tat' strategy against B in which zero transfers by B would be followed by zero transfers by A, and positive transfers by B would be followed by 'large' transfers by A, where 'large' means large enough to ensure that B would not gain by engaging in positive transfer activity against A. By following this rule, A defends, and thus creates, his right to the goods he has produced, and respects, and thus creates, B's rights to the goods that B has produced.

Now why should A stop there? Why should he not gain by going further and defend, and thus create, his right to transfer, unimpeded by B's protection activity, some of the goods produced by B? All that is needed is slight modification of A's rule, whereby A makes small, but nevertheless positive, transfers of goods produced by B in every period, but makes additional 'large' transfers to punish B if B transfers any of A's goods or protects his goods against A's small transfer.

If B fails to follow a rule of his own, there is indeed no reason why A should not thus gain by following a rule in which he collects tribute from B. A's capacity to collect tribute from B is limited only by his ability to impose on B punishment sufficiently severe that B prefers to pay tribute. In effect, A can make B his slave — having only those rights which it is in A's interests to grant him, which means none at all. The outcome of a game between a rational rule-following agent and one who does not follow rules would resemble that between master and dog, or a farmer and his cattle. It is to avoid this outcome that B too would choose to follow a rule, in which he defines for himself some rights by punishing transgressions. Only when *both* A and B follow rules to defend a boundary can there exist a boundary which lies between the two extremes in which A enslaves B or B enslaves A. Only in the case of such an interior equilibrium can we say that there is a social equilibrium in which both A and B have rights and so can be said to be members of society. Slaves are not members of society. Only an agent who follows rules is a member of society — is a person rather than a mere rational animal.

Let us then consider a game between two persons — between two members of society — who both follow rules to defend a boundary between their respective rights by punishing and hence deterring transgressions by the other. What is it that ensures that they both defend one and the same boundary — that their perceived boundaries coincide?

If a rule of action is to deter transgressions, that rule must impose costs on a transgressor equal to, or greater than, his benefits from transgressing. Faced with B following such a rule, A would then never claim rights which he expected B to defend, for by exercising those rights he would trigger punishment the costs of which would exceed the benefits of exercising those rights. Neither, however, would A fail to claim rights which B did not claim, for he could gain those rights without triggering punishment. The result then, is that A will rationally claim just those rights that he expects B not to defend. A will defend a boundary which lies exactly adjacent to the boundary he expects B to defend. Similarly B, knowing that A will follow a rule of punishing transgressions, will claim just those rights that he expects A not to defend.

The game between A and B in choosing a boundary is thus exactly like the following game: There is a fixed sum of money to be divided between two players. Each player submits a claim. If the sum of the claims does not exceed the total, then each gets what he claims and any remainder is thrown away. If there is an excess of the sum of the claims over the total, then each gets the total minus the others' claim, minus a small fraction of that excess.

We can represent this formally:

$$R_A = C_A \quad \text{if} \quad C_A + C_B \leqslant T \tag{6.1}$$

$$R_A = T - C_B - f(C_A + C_B - T) \quad \text{if} \quad C_A + C_B \geqslant T \tag{6.2}$$

where R_A is the payoff to A, C_A is A's claim, T is the total amount of money, and f is a small positive number. The same applies, *mutatis mutandis*, for player B. We can see that provided the sum of the claims does not exceed the total, A's returns are increasing in his claim, and otherwise are decreasing in his claim. A's optimal claim is thus the total minus B's claim. Similarly, B's optimal claim is the total minus A's claim. Each seeks to claim exactly what he expects the other not to claim. Each seeks to place a boundary exactly where he expects the other to do likewise. This then explains the players' incentives to co-ordinate their marking of boundaries — to ensure that their perceived boundaries coincide so that boundaries exist not merely subjectively, with each agent perceiving a different boundary, but as an intersubjective, and hence objective, social phenomenon. To draw an analogy between the distribution of rights and language, a particular line can be said to be *the* boundary between agents' rights only because it is widely perceived as such by members of the relevant community, just as the word 'dog' can be said to mean dog only because it is widely perceived to have that meaning in the relevant community.

The game described above has no unique equilibrium. Any pair of positive claims which sum to the total constitutes a Nash equilibrium to the game. Similarly the current distribution of rights is arbitrary. Similarly it is arbitrary that the word 'dog' rather than the word 'cat' is used to mean dog. How then do agents, even though they *wish* to co-ordinate their moves, actually *succeed* in doing so? How does A know how much B will claim, when there are many pairs of claims that are equilibria? Schelling (1960) answers this question by saying that the players will look for a 'focal point' — some prominent feature in an otherwise featureless landscape which can serve to pick out one of the many possible equilibria. An equal division of the sum of money might be just such a focal point of the above described game. A mountain range, or a river, or a line of latitude or longitude, might serve as a focal point for a boundary between nations. Above all, however, past practice itself may serve as a focal point par excellence. Whatever the historical reasons for using the word 'dog' to mean dog, given that the practice exists, who now would use the word 'cat' instead and expect to be understood? The choice of the 49th parallel as the boundary between Canada and the United States must have been arbitrary, but given the years of past practice, who would expect either country to claim and defend any other boundary? In a repeated game, once A and B have eventually settled on a pair of claims, C_A and C_B, which sum to the total amount of money T, why should A ever expect B to submit a different claim? Constant repetition makes an arbitrary equilibrium appear unique, and in a game of co-ordination, as all these games are, an equilibrium which appears unique is unique.

6.5   Conflicts, Crime, and Accidents

When the law is broken, the costs of apprehending the criminal, putting him on trial, and inflicting punishment, are often considerable. The value of any restitution he might make, and the chances that punishment might reform the criminal, are usually negligible. The crime, once done, cannot be undone. Why then is it rational to punish criminals? The answer is that it is rational to *follow a rule* of punishing, for the knowledge that one is following such a rule will deter future crimes. The act of punishing is not rational in itself. It is rational only as an instantiation of a rule of punishing. If the act of punishing were not performed, that would reveal that the rule of punishing were not being followed, and the capacity to deter criminals and to enforce the law would be lost.

A protagonist to a conflict could give (and often will give) exactly the same explanation of why it is rational for him to fight. Consider, for example, the Falklands War. It seems quite possible that the cost to Britain of retaking and subsequently defending the islands, in lives and money, exceeded the value of the islands themselves. This would have appeared even more plausible at the beginning of the war, when Britain's military success was not assured. Why then was it rational for Britain to fight the war? The answer could have been given, and was given, that if Britain failed to fight for her rights in this instance she would be inviting future aggression. Similarly, in an industrial dispute, the union or employer may argue that even though it is costly to pursue a strike, it must defend its rights now if it is to deter transgressions of its rights in future.

Any agent who wishes to have rights must ensure that violations of his rights are deterred by following a rule of imposing costs on those who violate his rights which exceed their gains. He will impose punishment even when it is costly to do so. The costs of carrying out an act of punishment are the price that must be paid to maintain one's reputation for punishing, and hence to maintain one's rights. The nation at war, or the union in a strike, is willing to bear the costs of conflict for exactly the same reason that 'society' is willing to bear the costs of punishing criminals.

We now understand, given that a right has been violated, why the injured party will rationally impose costs on the violator even if it is costly to do so. But this is only one half of the explanation of why costly conflicts occur. It takes (at least) two sides to make a conflict. If one side will rationally follow a rule which makes violations of his rights unprofitable, why should the other side then rationally violate his rights?

I have been constructing an analogy between a nation at war, or a union on strike, with a magistrate punishing a criminal. In terms of this analogy, we have explained why a magistrate should punish criminals even when it is costly to do so, and the question now becomes: why does crime exist? Why does the magistrate not impose punishment sufficiently severe to deter all crime? There is, I believe, no single answer to this question, but rather several possible answers, all depending on the existence of uncertainty so that being convicted of a crime can always be, to some extent, accidental.

Why, for instance, is life imprisonment not imposed for exceeding the speed limit? Presumably a penalty so severe would deter all speeding. The equilibrium that would then result would be ideal —

the law would be perfectly enforced and the costs of inflicting punishment would be zero, since punishment would never need to be imposed. This presumption is probably incorrect, however. The methods used by the police to measure speed can never be perfectly accurate, nor can the reliability of witnesses, judges and juries be perfect. Some innocent drivers will always be falsely convicted for speeding, so the penalty *would* be imposed in equilibrium, and the costs of inflicting such a penalty would be high (both on the victim and on the rest of society). Also, the methods used by drivers to monitor their own speeds are equally inaccurate, and additional accuracy can only be achieved at a cost. Faced with such a severe penalty, drivers may drive well below the official speed limit, leaving a large margin for error, thus nullifying the law's objectives. Alternatively, drivers would invest in very accurate, and hence very costly speedometers, and spend most of their time watching their speedometers and speed limit signs. Furthermore, it is recognized that there may be emergencies when it is quite legitimate for drivers to break the speed limit, but it is costly to specify and publicize in advance exactly what emergencies would constitute a valid defence against a charge of speeding. Faced with a too severe penalty, drivers would not exceed the speed limit even when it was desirable for them to do so. A more moderate penalty would make it more likely that the driver's cost–benefit calculus would more nearly match the social trade-off.

In sum, it is costly to define the law precisely, costly for the magistrate to know with certainty whether the law has been broken, and costly for the potential criminal to know with certainty whether an action he takes will result in his breaking the law. With an overly severe penalty, either the costs of perfect accuracy must be borne, or else the costs of actually inflicting the penalty must be borne. The optimal penalty will generally be less than the maximum possible. It will be desirable to trade off a higher frequency of crime and punishment for a lower cost of precision and lower cost per episode of punishment. This is most clearly seen if we assume that there exists some positive lower bound to the frequency of crime, so that some crime will always exist even under the most draconian penalties. At such a bound, a reduction in the severity of punishment would have a non-negligible effect on the cost per episode of punishment, but a negligible effect on the frequency of punishment episodes, thus reducing the product of the two, which is the total costs of inflicting punishment.[3]

Conflict between two nations at war, or between union and employer in a strike, is simply a two-sided version of the game between magistrate and criminal. Each side plays magistrate to the other's criminal. Each side sees itself as punishing the other for violating its rights. Even though it is costly for both sides to engage in mutual punishment, just as it is costly for the magistrate to punish the criminal, each must act as if committed to following its rule of punishing what is perceived as violations of its rights. An observed failure to bear these costs would result in a loss of reputation for following that rule, and with this would come the loss of deterrence of future violations, and with that would come the loss of ability to enforce its rights and hence the loss of those rights themselves. The reason why parties to a conflict, each perceiving the other to have violated its rights, fail to make the mutually beneficial exchange that would terminate the costly conflict, is simply that they *cannot* do so. Any exchange is an exchange of rights, and rights must be enforced by rules of action, and those very rules of action require each side not to let the other gain by violating his rights. A retreat in the face of a transgression of the boundary merely rewards that transgression, and so encourages future transgressions of whichever new boundary retreated to and where the costs of punishing must be borne, or else all rights will be lost. The agent facing conflict can no more *always* accept a compromise settlement than a magistrate can *always* tell convicted criminals that he will not punish them if they promise not to do it again.

Conflicts, like crime, occur because information is costly and so people make mistakes. Consider two agents, each enforcing a common boundary which marks their respective rights. Neither will knowingly transgress that boundary because each knows that the other is following a rule of punishing transgressions which ensures that the transgressor does not gain from his action. Suppose, however, that the exact location of the boundary is uncertain (or, which amounts to the same thing, that neither has perfectly accurate information on whether he, or the other, has transgressed the boundary). Given such uncertainty, it may happen that the two agents have different expectations as to the location of the boundary, so that some rights are claimed by both agents. In such a case, in exercising what he perceives as his rights, each is perceived by the other as violating the other's rights. Each must implement his rule of action to punish this perceived violation. Each must ensure that the other does not gain by this perceived violation. A must ensure that B is no better off than if he had accepted A's definition of the boundary. B similarly must ensure that A is no better off than if he had accepted B's definition of the boundary. Neither can accept a compromise boundary because to do so would be to reward and encourage future encroachments. Given their rules of action it necessarily follows that the total costs of mutual punishment are at least equal to the value of the disputed rights. It is as if conflicts were a ritual in which that which is disputed is ceremonially destroyed in order to discourage further disputes.

Suppose it were possible to draw a sharp distinction between accidental and deliberate violations of rights. (It is not generally possible to do so because the frequency of accidents can generally be reduced, but at a cost.) Accidental violations, by definition, are those which cannot be deterred, and so agents would not wish to engage in costly punishment of accidental violations. They would however wish to punish deliberate violations — those which can be deterred. If agents were able to distinguish independently those disputes which arise from an accidental difference in opinion from those which arise from a deliberate attempt by one party to claim rights he knows to belong to the other, then no conflicts would ever occur. Accidental disputes would be settled by a compromise, and deliberate violations would be punished sufficiently severely to deter them. Conflicts occur because agents cannot distinguish accidental from deliberate disputes. Even if punishment were sufficiently severe to deter all deliberate violations, so that both sides would know that all actual conflicts arose from an accidental and honest difference of opinion as to who is violating whose rights, they cannot act on this knowledge, and negotiate a compromise, without simultaneously destroying the very basis for that knowledge, for to fail to punish would be to invite deliberate violations. To practice 'splitting the difference' between claims, for instance, is to give others the incentive to claim, and eventually to get, all your rights.

To illustrate the costs of conflict, consider again the simple game described in the previous section, where the players' returns are a function of their claims as defined by equations (6.1) and (6.2). These functions define a solution to a problem posed by Conrad in *Typhoon*, where the Captain must somehow redistribute to their original owners a large quantity of coins that had become mixed together following a storm at sea, and must somehow induce the owners to tell the truth about how many coins each owns. If each expects the others to claim exactly what they own, then it is optimal for him to claim exactly what he owns. Though there are many other possible equilibria to this game, the equilibrium where each claims exactly what he owns is the most natural 'focal point' of the game.

If none of the coins has been lost, and each remembers exactly how many coins he owned, the outcome is exactly as desired, with each getting exactly the number of coins he previously owned. Suppose however that, unnoticed by anyone, some of the coins had been lost during the storm. If each then claims what he believes he owns, the sum of the claims will exceed the total number of remaining coins. Assume for simplicity two players, each originally owning 50 coins, and that 10 coins have been lost. Each claims 50, and gets slightly less than 40 coins (the total of 90, minus the other's claim of 50, minus the small 'fine' of the fraction 'f' times the excess claim of 10). The remaining coins, slightly more than 10, are thrown overboard. These 10 coins thrown overboard represent the deadweight costs of conflict, in which the disputed property is destroyed. There is no way, however, to avoid the possibility of such costs while retaining each player's incentive to submit an honest claim. They can only be minimized by making the rate of fine, 'f', as small as possible (but still positive).

6.6 Strikes

Let us now illustrate this theory of conflict by applying it to the case of strikes. It is understood here that the word 'strike' is used to refer to both strikes and lock-outs. Which side takes the first step in breaking the exchange of labour for money is immaterial. It takes two sides to make a conflict. Each refuses to accept the other's offer and to make an offer acceptable to the other, so that there is always joint responsibility for the conflict, regardless of whether it is called a strike or a lock-out.

A strike is a disruption of a trading relationship between workers and employer, but not all disruptions of trading relationships are strikes. Holidays and sick-leave, for example, also constitute a temporary cessation of trade between workers and employers. What sets strikes apart from these and other disruptions is that strikes are perceived to be mutually costly — an absence of trade when trade could be mutually beneficial — and that strikes are disputes about the terms of trade — the level of wages, other benefits and working conditions. Since other benefits and working conditions can generally be translated into a monetary equivalent, we shall, for simplicity, speak of strikes as being solely concerned with the level of wages.

If labour markets operated like the frictionless and perfectly competitive model of the textbooks, strikes would not be possible, because a disruption of trade between any particular employer and worker would not be costly. The level of wages (making due allowance for other benefits and working conditions) would have to equal the level set by the market for that particular type of worker. If one employer set wages below the market level, all his employees would immediately quit to work for other employers. If one group of workers demanded wages above the market level, their employer would immediately fire them and replace them with others. With costless substitution of trading partners, a separation between any two partners imposes no costs. A necessary condition for strikes, then, is that substitution of trading partners be costly, or impossible, so that a temporary separation leaves both partners single.

For various reasons substitution of trading partners in the labour market is generally costly, so that the relation between worker and employer is more like a marriage than a one night stand. There are joint rents to continuing the relationship between two particular partners which are lost if that relationship is temporarily suspended, as in a strike. The relationship is, to at least some extent, one of bilateral monopoly. Such a bilateral monopoly may be natural, or it may be deliberately created by one or other trading partner, or by legislation.

A bilateral monopoly may arise naturally, for example, for reasons of geography. Many isolated mining towns have only a single employer. More commonly, however, labour markets are characterized by costless substitutability *ex ante* but costly substitutability *ex post*. Before the trading relation begins, employer and worker both have a wide choice of highly substitutable potential trading partners. But as soon as a choice is made the worker acquires specific human capital — special skills and knowledge that are useful with this employer, but not with any other — and puts down roots in other ways as well. For either side subsequently to switch partners would mean these partner-specific investments would become valueless and need to be expensively reacquired.[4]

Even when there are no such naturally occurring costs of substituting trading partners, such costs may be artificially created in order to give one partner monopoly power over the other. A union will generally go to considerable lengths to prevent an employer from temporarily or permanently substituting 'scabs' for striking workers. Their power to do so is supplemented by popular opinion and sometimes by government legislation, as in the Canadian province of Quebec at the time of writing. The opposite case, where employers 'blacklist' striking employees to prevent them from working elsewhere, has also occasionally been seen. A union which thus creates monopoly power for itself by coercing its partner into 'faithfulness', also creates monopsony power for its partner too, for if wages are thus raised above the competitive level the worker who switches to another employer will suffer a drop in wages. (And if all groups of workers follow the same strategy, so that wages are everywhere above the competitive level and an excess supply of labour results, the worker may be unable to find another employer and the alternative to his current partner will be unemployment.)

For any of these above reasons then, labour markets are typically characterized by some degree of bilateral monopoly. The alternative to continuing trade with the existing partner is either a costly switch to an alternative partner, or not to trade at all. The lowest wage at which the worker would find it just profitable to continue the relationship (the worker's 'reservation wage') may be well below the highest wage at which the employer would find it just profitable to continue the relationship (the employer's reservation wage). This gap between workers' and employers' reservation wages measures the joint rents to their relationship, and it is the loss of these rents that constitutes the joint costs of a strike. With costless substitutability of partners in a perfectly competitive market, the two reservation wages would coincide and equal the market wage, and strikes would be costless, irrelevant, and so would not exist.

We know that actual wages must lie between the employer's and worker's reservation wages, for otherwise one or other side will terminate the relationship. But where within this zone of indeterminacy will wages actually lie? How will firm and worker divide these joint rents to their relationship?

One answer, again following Hicks (1964), asserts that the division of these rents, or the level of wages, is determined by the relative bargaining power of the two sides. Though what determines this relative bargaining power is not well understood, at least in the case of symmetrical partners one should find a symmetrical solution — one which divides the rents equally. As I have argued in section 6.3, however, there are good reasons why agents should not want the distribution of rights — in this case the level of wages — to be determined solely by their relative bargaining power. If wages were determined in this manner, each would have an incentive to invest resources in an attempt to change the level of wages in the desired direction. For example, workers would avoid buying houses and taking other decisions which would reduce their mobility and their reservation wages, and hence also reducing their actual wages. Similarly, the employer would spend money to make him less reliant on particular workers, in order to reduce his reservation wage. In general, each will invest less in a relationship if the joint returns are split between both and each only obtains one-half of the total return to an investment he makes. For these reasons, as well as others, both would prefer wages to be determined by some form of contractual understanding, so that wages are independent of bargaining power and the incentives for each to spend money to gain at the other's expense are eliminated. I believe this is the primary reason for wages being determined by contract rather than bargaining power alone, though other considerations, such as the optimal sharing of risks between firm and worker, may also play a part.

If a contract is to be feasible, however, it must nevertheless set wages somewhere between the firm's and the worker's reservation wages, for otherwise one or other party would not willingly trade at the contractual wage, and the contract would become unenforceable. Since both reservation wages will tend to move over time with market conditions, in a way that cannot accurately be predicted, a contract which simply fixed wages for the prospective lifetime of the trading relation would, sooner or later, become unenforceable as the contractual wage moved outside the zone bordered by the two reservation wages. The problem is to find a contract which makes the contractual wage contingent on the reservation wages, to preserve enforceability, and yet exogenous to manipulation by firm and worker, to prevent mutually costly rent-seeking. The solution is to find a set of 'instrumental variables' — variables which are correlated with the natural movements of the two reservation wages but are exogenous to firm and worker, and which make contractual wages contingent on those variables. Likely examples of such instrumental variables are the levels of wages elsewhere, the price level, the rate of unemployment, conditions in the firm's output market, etc.

Contracts motivated by optimal risk-sharing, of course, would also in general require the contractual wage to be made contingent on other variables, such as the consumer price index and the firm's output price. For whatever reason, we shall assume a contract which sets wages contingent on other variables, which we shall call 'conditioning variables'.

It may be costly to set down such a contract in writing in such a form that it would be enforced by third parties, especially if it is to cover what is to be paid in all eventualities, many of which are very unlikely to arise. It may also be costly for third parties to monitor some conditioning variables which the firm and worker learn about as a matter of course in their general activities. For this reason, the contract may be left implicit or unwritten, and hence be enforceable only by firm and worker themselves.

If this view is correct, then the explicit contracts we see negotiated at intervals of one to three years are not independent and original contracts in their own right, but are merely *interpretations* of a much longer-term implicit contract. The relation between these short-term explicit contracts and the underlying long-term implicit contract is similar to the relation between a particular ruling by a judge and the tradition of common law. Each explicit contract is merely an interpretation of the implicit contract, and yet, at the same time, the implicit contract is nothing but a theoretical entity constructed out of the history of precedents set by past explicit contracts, for which it provides a theoretical understanding by imposing coherence and continuity.

The key point is that the short-term explicit contracts we observe are not negotiated in a vacuum, mindless of history. In the haggling that precedes the signing of an explicit contract, firm and workers are trying to interpret an implicit contract to see what levels of wages it specifies for the current period, given the current values of the conditioning variables. Each side must defend its contractual rights and enforce the contract, for if it fails to do so it will lose any share of the joint rents. It defends its rights and enforces the contract by following a rule requiring it to punish what it perceives as violations of the contract severely enough so that the violator does not profit from his violation, and future violations are deterred. The most obvious way to impose punishment is simply to withdraw from trade.

Suppose the workers, represented by a union, believe that given current circumstances the wage specified by the implicit contract is some level $W_u(0)$. If the union is to ensure that the firm does not gain by insisting on a lower wage, the union must make the firm 'pay' for concessions by suffering a strike. The maximum rate at which the union can concede without rewarding the firm for violating the contract is that at which at all points along its concession curve, $W_u(s)$, the firm's rents if it pays a wage $W_u(s)$ after a strike of length s, equal the rents it would get if it paid $W_u(0)$ with no strike.

Similarly, if the firm believes that the implicit contract specifies a wage $W_F(0)$, then the maximum rate at which it can concede without rewarding the union for violating the contract is that at which all points on its concession curve, $W_F(s)$, the workers' rents if they accept a wage $W_F(s)$ after a strike of length s, equal the rents they would get had they accepted $W_F(0)$ with no strike. Faced with the other side following a rule of conceding at slightly less than these maximum rates, each side will effectively be deterred from deliberately trying to violate the contract.

If both sides form the same opinion as to the contractual wage, so that $W_u(0)$ equals $W_F(0)$, no strike will result. Given the very nature of the implicit contract, however, and the fact that the two sides may have slightly different information on the conditioning variables, on which the contractual wage is contingent, it is no surprise that their honest opinions as to the contractual wage may differ. If they differ so that $W_u(0)$ exceeds $W_F(0)$, where each thinks the other is demanding more than his due, then the rules of action followed by each to enforce the contract make a strike inevitable. The length of strike and the settlement wage are determined by the intersection of the two concession curves.

By making some simplifying assumption, we can mathematically derive the two concession curves and solve for the settlement wage and strike length. Assume that the current explicit contract will last for one period and will create no precedents for future explicit contracts, and that the rate of interest is zero. If V is the firm's reservation wage then the left hand side of 6.3 represents the firm's rents over the remainder of the period if it accepts the union's demand $W_u(s)$ after a strike of length s. The right hand side represents the firm's rents if it accepts the union's initial demand with no strike. In setting the two equal we are assuming that the union concedes at the maximum possible rate consistent with not rewarding the firm for failing to accept its initial demand.

$$(V - W_u(s))(1 - s) = V - W_u(0) \qquad (6.3)$$

If U is the workers' reservation wage, then a comparable equation for holding the workers' rents constant is:

$$(W_F(s) - U)((1 - s) = W_F(0) - U \qquad (6.4)$$

Equations (6.3) and (6.4) can be rearranged to find the union's and firm's concession curves:

$$W_u(s) = \frac{W_u(0) - sV}{1 - s} \qquad (6.5)$$

$$W_F(s) = \frac{W_F(0) - sU}{1 - s} \tag{6.6}$$

It can be verified that both firm and union concede as the strike progresses (the firm raising its wage offer and the union reducing its wage demand), and that both concede at an increasing rate. The strike ends when it reaches a length S^*, such that the firm's wage offer coincides with the union's wage demand, which determine the settlement wage W^*.

$$W^* = W_F(S^*) = W_u(S^*) \tag{6.7}$$

The strike length is thus given by:

$$S^* = \frac{W_u(0) - W_F(0)}{V - U} \tag{6.8}$$

It can be seen that the length of strike is directly proportional to the difference between the initial demands, and inversely proportional to the costs per period of a strike.

The settlement is most usefully expressed as the division of the remaining rents after the strike:

$$\frac{V - W^*}{W^* - U} = \frac{V - W_u(0)}{W_F(0) - U} \tag{6.9}$$

They divide the remaining pie in the proportions that the other thinks each deserves.

The occasional occurrence of strikes can thus be seen as a result of rules of action followed rationally by firm and worker to enforce a long-term implicit contract which sets a wage contingent on imperfectly observed variables. These rules of action, by punishing dishonest claims, provide a mechanism which gives each side an incentive to reveal honestly its partially private information on those variables and hence on the contractual wage. Given these rules of action, strikes will occur when the two sides receive different information so that each side believes it deserves more than the other believes it deserves. The result of the strike is that each side gets no more than the other side believes it deserves. The remainder is destroyed.

Though it must never be allowed to get more, each side may in fact get less than the other believes it deserves. The concession curves described above, which ensure that each side neither gains nor loses from a perceived violation, will just barely deter deliberate violations only if all such violations are detected. But in order for strikes actually to occur with a positive probability, the two sides' information must be at least partially independent, but this in turn implies that monitoring of violations must be imperfect. Suppose for instance that the implicit contract requires the wage to be contingent on the firm's output price, a high price requiring a high wage, and that the firm observes its output price perfectly, but the workers observe this price only imperfectly. Suppose the firm observes a high price, but dishonestly claims the price is low and so offers only a low wage. In doing so, the firm takes into account that there is a small probability that its dishonesty may not be detected — if the workers are misinformed and believe that the price really is low. If crime is imperfectly monitored, so that criminals are not caught with certainty, the costs of punishment to the criminal must exceed his benefits, in order that the expected costs equal the expected benefits and crime be deterred. This means that the rates of concession must be slower, and so strikes longer and more costly, than was stated in the equations above, as the two sides' information becomes less than perfectly correlated. The less perfectly correlated are the two sides' honest beliefs as to the contractual wage, the more frequent will be the occurrence of strikes, and the slower will be the rates at which the two sides concede during the strike.

Any theory of strikes which yields predictions about the length of a strike and the settlement wage, as this one does, must answer the following question. As soon as the strike begins, why do both sides not do what is mutually advantageous and immediately agree to resume trading at that predicted settlement wage? This theory can answer that question confidently. If either side were to make such a concession, it would immediately lose its reputation for following a rule of action whereby it punishes perceived violations of the contract. It would thus encourage future violations and be unable to enforce the contract. Neither side can concede so quickly that it fails to deter deliberate violations of the contract. To concede more slowly than this, on the other hand, would be to increase the costs of conflict to both needlessly, for deterrence would be more than assured. Given that each adopts a strategy that just deters deliberate violations, all strikes are the result of accidental violations of the contract, but must be treated as if they were deliberate in order not to encourage deliberate violations.

6.7   The Limitation and Containment of Conflicts

A conflict is limited if it ends before the complete capitulation, or loss of power to continue the conflict, by one or other side. A conflict is contained if one or both sides foregoes the use of apparently effective weapons that it is able to use against the other.

Strikes are nearly always limited in this sense. They nearly always end with some sort of compromise between the two sides' initial offers, and both sides will return again to the bargaining table in future negotiations. They are also virtually always highly contained. The weapons used are nearly always restricted to the withdrawal from trade itself. Only rarely does the conflict spill over into other forms of mutually costly behaviour.

Other forms of conflict, such as wars, more often are unlimited — ending only in the total victory of one side or the other — and are less contained, though even here it is perhaps surprising that nations with the capability to do so do not use poison gas and nuclear weapons more often. It may be, of course, that we reserve the word 'wars' for those conflicts that are less limited and less contained than others, but the question still remains as to why some conflicts are more limited and more contained than are others.

Let us first examine what determines whether conflicts are limited or unlimited. When A perceives B to have violated A's rights, A must impose punishment on B if he is to maintain his rights by deterring future violations. In punishing B, however, A may well be violating B's rights, which in turn would require B to punish A to maintain his rights, and so on. Each successive round of punishment sparks a further round of retaliation. Suppose, for instance, that the original cause of the conflict is that A perceives B to have stolen some of A's goods, and A then punishes B by stealing some of B's goods (fining B for his crime). Under what conditions will the successive rounds of punishment get smaller and smaller and eventually die out, and under what conditions will they get larger and larger and the conflict escalate until one or other side is forced to capitulate — when the costs of continuing the conflict exceed the value of his reputation for protecting his rights? The answer depends on the value of two critical ratios, which we may call the deterrence ratio and the punishment cost ratio.

Suppose A perceives B to have violated A's rights, and punishes B in retaliation. Let B_B represent B's benefits from committing the perceived violation, C_B be the cost imposed on B by A's punishment, and B_A (which may be negative) be the benefits to A of punishing B. Then A's deterrence ratio, d_A, and punishment cost ratio, P_A, are defined as:

$$d_A = \frac{C_B}{B_B} \qquad\qquad (6.10)$$

$$P_A = \frac{B_A}{C_B} \qquad\qquad (6.11)$$

The product of the two ratios gives the ratio of A's benefits from punishing B to B's benefits from violating A's rights.

$$d_A P_A = \frac{B_A}{B_B} \qquad\qquad (6.12)$$

Now, if the product of the two ratios is positive, so that A gets positive benefits from punishing B, then B in turn must punish A for punishing B. If he were to fail to do so, he would give A an incentive to claim falsely that B has violated A's rights, in order to reap the benefits that accrue for punishing B for his alleged crime. Thus if the product of A's two ratios proves positive, a second round of punishment will occur. The product of B's deterrence and punishment cost ratios will, in turn, yield the ratio of B's benefits from punishing A to A's benefits from punishing B. The product of the four ratios yields the benefits gained by B from inflicting retaliatory punishment on A divided by B's benefits from the original perceived crime. If the product of the four ratios is less than one, each successive round of punishment will get smaller and smaller and the total costs of conflict will reach a finite limit. If on the other hand, the product exceeds one, successive rounds of punishment will get larger and larger and the conflict will be unlimited.

The two deterrence ratios can never be less than one, for the costs of punishment must be greater than the benefits from crime if crime is to be deterred. If the detection of crime is imperfect, or if the policeman is uncertain of the criminal's costs and benefits and wishes to be sure that crime will be deterred, then the deterrence ratio may considerably exceed one. The punishment cost ratio, on the other hand, cannot exceed one, and may well be negative (if it is costly to impose punishment on another). If negative, the conflict will stop after the first round, for A does not gain by punishing B so there is no incentive for him to falsely accuse B, and hence no need for B to retaliate. The reason the punishment cost ratio cannot exceed one is that if it did so there would have existed unexploited gains from trade, for before the conflict A would willingly have paid B sufficient compensation to sell his rights and grant A the right to 'punish' B. Whether or not conflicts are unlimited, therefore, depends on whether the product of four ratios, two of which exceed one, the other two being less than one, exceeds one. Either case is possible. If the parties wish to limit the size of the conflict, however, they will rationally take care to ensure that they do not impose punishment more severe than is needed for deterrence, and will also deliberately choose methods of punishment which are costly to the person who imposes punishment, not merely costly to the person on whom punishment is imposed.

This insight might explain why strikes are nearly always limited, and also why nearly all conflicts are contained in the sense that some apparently effective weapons are not used.

In punishing a perceived crime, the policeman must somehow signal that what he is doing is punishing a perceived crime, and not benefiting by committing a crime himself — which could spark retaliation. By following a rule agents perform acts that are ir-rational, except in so far as their performance is necessary to maintain agents' reputations for following that rule. If an act of punishing is costly to the policeman, and conspicuously so, then it can only be understood as being an act of punishment — rational only as an instantiation of a rule of action the following of which creates rights. Saying 'this hurts me as well as hurting you' implies that you are punishing, and your action cannot be interpreted as motivated by mere expediency, but instead by the principle of a rule. Strikes are limited conflicts because the method by which punishment is inflicted, withdrawing from trade, conspicuously imposes costs on both sides. Strikes are rational precisely because they are so conspicuously irrational — except, of course, to agents who rationally want them to be seen thus. For the very same reason, nations at war may refrain from using nuclear weapons, even if one or both sides possesses a nuclear capability, provided there is a reasonable expectation that the conflict will remain limited if such weapons are not used. They refrain from using nuclear weapons precisely because they are such a cost-effective weapon — being cheap to use and giving the user a decided military advantage they cannot but provoke further punishment for their use. In small wars, where the rights in dispute are not large, and the opponent is too powerful to be destroyed at a stroke, it is wise to ensure that operations against the enemy cost your side some lives and material as well as your enemy's. This may also explain why courts impose prison sentences rather than fines, even though monetary fines appear an ideally efficient way of imposing punishment. It is precisely because fines are so efficient, yielding benefits to the rest of society equal to their costs to the criminal, and so having a punishment cost ratio of one, that they are not always imposed. To rely on fines is to create the incentive for deliberately convicting the innocent to fill the state's coffers.

6.8   Conflicts Preserve Consensus

What we might call 'the social order' rests on a lattice of imaginary lines. These lines, as boundaries, borders, or contracts, delineate or define what is rightfully one agent's or rightfully another's; they define what actions each agent has the right to perform. The position of these lines is largely arbitrary. It is determined by history rather than current circumstances. The only reason these imaginary lines can be said to exist at all is that agents in society act as if they did exist. They rarely cross these lines, so their position can be inferred by an outside observer only by observing the behaviour of those agents to see where they do or do not trespass. The amazing fact is that virtually all agents nearly always seem to agree as to the exact location of these imaginary and arbitrarily positioned lines. It is only because of this fact that it is meaningful to speak of a social order at all. What maintains this agreement as to the location of these lines are the actions taken when disagreement occurs and a breach appears in the common knowledge of the location of these lines. In such instances, agents engage in mutually costly behaviour which we call conflict. What this conflict does is to destroy the land which lies within the zone of ambiguity, thereby preserving agreement over what remains and closing the breach.

Notes

1. The Hicksian diagram which shows the employer's and union's concession curves with wage on one axis and expected duration of strike on the other axis, does not, contrary to initial impressions, determine actual or expected strike length by the intersection of the two curves. Rather, the intersection of the two curves (which show the wage each side would accept *instead of* a *threatened* strike, as a function of the length of that strike) is said to determine the wage the two sides will agree on without the threatened strike actually taking place.
2. Umbeck (1981), for example, argues that 'might makes rights' and that the distribution of ownership of land will be determined by equality at the margin of the agent's benefits from owning land and costs of enforcing his claim. With the smoothly diminishing marginal net returns assumed, the margin should be continuously moving with changing exogenous circumstances, and so too should the boundary, which it doesn't.
3. Stigler (1970) presents an alternative explanation of why penalties are not maximally severe. If all crimes carried the same maximum penalty, then criminals would substitute away from lesser into greater crimes, preferring to risk being hanged for a sheep than for a lamb, which is to society's detriment. If the worst crime carries the maximally severe penalty, lesser crimes will need lesser penalties. Unfortunately, Stigler's answer is incomplete, for it begs the crucial question of whether maximally severe penalties on all crimes would deter all crime, so that

criminals would rather be hanged for a sheep than for a lamb, but better still would rather steal neither.

4. Okun (1981) likens these costs to those of the individual worker and employer having to pay an initial 'toll' before they are permitted to trade but, having paid once, they need never pay again, unless they switch to another trading partner.

7

Concluding Remarks on Altruism and Egoism

Questions such as 'how is society possible?' make little or no sense when asked in a theoretical vacuum, just as the question 'How are pandas possible?' makes no sense until we discover that the questioner is a Darwinian biologist asking how pandas could survive with a digestive system apparently so ill-adapted to their main source of food. Asked in a theoretical vacuum, to question how something is possible merely invites the reply: 'Why not?'

If one starts with the premise that 'man is by nature a social animal' (whatever that might exactly mean) then to ask how society is possible is either senseless, or else rather an awkward way of asking why man exists or why man is by nature social. The existence of society is only problematic when we start with the premise that 'man is *not* by nature social'. We ask how something is possible only when we accept a theoretical outlook which, if true, would seem prime facie to suggest that it is not possible, and we are trying to reconcile that theoretical outlook with the fact of the thing's existence. I start from the theoretical premise that each individual's behaviour is rationally chosen to pursue his own self-interest, and it is this premise that defines the problem I address and makes it interesting. How can the interaction of several individuals create something which the action of a single individual logically can not? Why should the patterns of ink on paper, which we call contracts, and the imaginary lines in space, which demarcate what we call property rights, rule the life of 'homo economicus' more completely than astrological portents rule the superstitious and cracks in paving stones rule the neurotic? How does the interaction of purely selfish individuals create not a Hobbesian war of all against all, but instead a society which, though imperfect, is nevertheless not so imperfect as to make immediately derisible and incredible the Functionalist thesis that those social institutions arise which best serve human needs? Given rational, self-interested, individual behaviour, society is at least problematic, if not downright paradoxical.

One answer to this paradox would, of course, be to reject the theoretical premise of rational, self-interested, individual behaviour. Might not our task be a lot easier if we started instead from a premise of irrational, or altruistic, or collective behaviour?

Rational behaviour and selfish behaviour are different and logically independent concepts. Behaviour can be rational and selfish, rational and unselfish, irrational and selfish, or irrational and unselfish. Rationality pertains to whether an agent's behaviour is likely (given his information) actually to promote his objectives, and selfishness pertains to whether the objectives he intends to promote include only his own interests or those of others as well.

Why have I assumed that human behaviour is self-regarding or selfish? The answer is *not* that I believe that all human behaviour is always wholly selfish. Instead, the answer is that I believe that human behaviour is on the whole *imperfectly* altruistic, and that interaction between imperfectly altruistic agents is qualitatively the same as interaction between purely selfish agents, and both are qualitatively quite different from the interaction between perfectly altruistic agents. What matters is not selfishness or altruism *per se*, but whether agents do, or do not, share identical ends. A perfectly altruistic agent (in the sense in which I use the term) considers another agent's interests as having an exactly equal importance to his own. Two perfectly altruistic agents, therefore, will share exactly the same objective, since each seeks to maximize the sum of his own and the other agent's personal utilities. Each will want to do exactly the same thing as the other would want him to do. Their interaction is that of a team, seeking a shared team objective. Their problem is not of conflicting objectives, but only of communicating information between them, and of co-ordinating their actions when no unique optimum exists (do we both drive on the right or on the left side of the road?). With perfect communication two altruists would choose actions unanimously, in the literal sense. They could be modelled as if having a single mind.

Leaving aside asymmetric cases, such as where one agent is purely selfish and the other cares only for the first agent's personal interest and not at all for his own, anything less than perfect altruism, so that each cares more for himself than for the other, will mean that their objectives do not perfectly coincide, and each will not always do what the other would want him to do. Their objectives will conflict to some extent, and the outcome of their interaction will not be unanimously optimal. There are then irreducibly two agents. If our interest is in human *inter*action, rather than simply human action, it is quite beside the point to debate whether altruistic behaviour is 'really' the selfish behaviour of those who happen to take pleasure in seeing others pleased. What matters is not the *source* of an agent's objective or utility function, but whether his objectives coincide with others'. Agents who, after discussion, typically pursue objectives identical to each other we call altruists. Agents who typically pursue quite different objectives (even from those we have previously decided to call altruists), we call selfish. My assumption of agents as selfish is no more than a way of assuming that their objectives do not coincide.

If all agents shared exactly the same objectives, as would happen if all were perfectly altruistic, then any optimal outcome is also a Nash equilibrium, since no agent would ever wish to move away from an outcome which was jointly optimal. When agents do not all share exactly the same objectives, as happens when they are more or less selfish, this result is changed in two ways. Firstly, we cannot speak of an outcome being optimal simpliciter, since what is most preferred by one agent will not usually be most preferred by all others. We must instead speak of outcomes being Pareto Optimal (or efficient) — being those outcomes where it is not possible to make one agent better off without making another worse off. Secondly, only by chance will any Pareto Optimal outcome be a Nash equilibrium since, with different objectives, at least one agent will usually gain by moving away from a Pareto Optimal outcome (though his doing so will hurt others), and if so that outcome cannot be a Nash equilibrium.

These points can be illustrated by the following simple example. Let there be two agents, A and B. Call A's chosen action X, and B's chosen action Y, where X and Y are continuous variables. Each agent's utility depends both on his own choice and on the other's choice of action. Let A's most preferred outcome be for him to choose an action X^a, and for B to choose an action Y^a, this outcome being represented then by the point $\{X^a, Y^a\}$. Similarly, let B's most preferred outcome be the point $\{X^b, Y^b\}$. If each agent gets less and less utility as he moves away from his most preferred point, then his indifference curves (connecting points of equal utility) will be roughly circular, with the most preferred point at the centre. The set

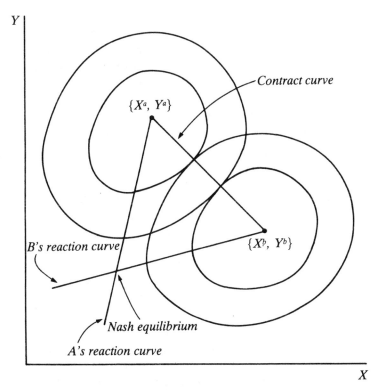

Figure 7.1

of Pareto Optimal points will lie on a line (called the 'contract curve') between the two agents' most preferred points, where their indifference curves are tangent to each other. A's 'reaction curve' shows his best choice of action as a function of a given action by B. It is found by joining together all the points where his indifference curves are exactly horizontal. Similarly, B's reaction curve is found by joining together all the points where B's indifference curves are vertical. The Nash equilibrium is at the intersection of the two reaction curves, a point where each agent's action is his best response to the other's action. See Figure 7.1.

If the two agents do not share the same objectives, then their most preferred points (and their indifference curves as a whole) will not coincide. The Nash equilibrium will not lie on the contract curve, and so will not be Pareto Optimal. Now imagine the two agents' objectives coming closer and closer together, so that A's most preferred point, and its associated indifference curves, moves closer and closer to B's most preferred point. As this occurs we notice two things happening. First, the contract curve shrinks, until it eventually becomes the jointly most preferred point. Second, the Nash equilibrium moves closer and closer to the contract curve, and hits the contract curve at exactly the same time as the latter becomes a point, which is when the two agents' objectives themselves exactly coincide. When the objectives of the two agents coincide, it is as if there were but a single agent choosing both actions.

Now, if it is hard to see how purely selfish individuals *could* have created social institutions which would appear to promote a more or less Pareto Optimal outcome, it is harder still to see why purely altruistic individuals should ever *need* to do so. As David Hume (1777, p. 186) argued so eloquently, the institution of private property rights would be quite redundant if all agents were perfectly altruistic for, sharing identical objectives, none would ever want to trespass on another's rights except in cases where the owner wanted him to do so. If private property rights did ever exist among perfectly altruistic agents, each would immediately wish to grant all other agents blanket permission to transgress his rights at the other's discretion, which permission would effectively imply the dissolution of all such rights. Similarly, the institution of promising would be redundant, for if it were optimal to perform the promised action the promisor would do so regardless of having undertaken an obligation to do so, and were it not optimal to perform it, the promisee would in any case willingly release him from his obligation. There are only two purposes that might be served by laws in a world populated entirely by perfect altruists. Firstly, laws might be a way for wiser and better informed altruists to advise their more stupid and ignorant brethren on the best actions to choose. Secondly, laws might enable altruists to co-ordinate their actions in a world where there is more than one optimum, but hitting it requires all agents to decide to aim for the same one, just as linguistic conventions enable us to agree on which words mean what. But such laws would be so unlike our existing laws as to be barely laws at all, but more like directives — rules of thumb designed for the pragmatic purpose of helping people better to achieve those ends they already seek, like a recipe for baking a cake. Threat of punishment would be quite unnecessary to enforce those laws.

Now, I have argued that social institutions are none other than the rules of action that agents choose to follow in contexts where their optimal plans are time-inconsistent, and it is surely more than a mere coincidence that, just as our existing social institutions would be superfluous in a world of perfect altruists, so too the problem of time-inconsistency of optimal plans could not arise! Time-inconsistency arises because when an agent can precommit his action he will use this ability to influence other agents actions by influencing their expectations of his future action. But if all agents are perfect altruists, and so share an identical objective, none would need to influence the actions of others, since they would in any case be planning to do exactly what he wants them to do. More formally, in terms of the mathematical example of time-inconsistency given in Chapter 3, the second term in equation 3.4 will be zero, since $\delta U/\delta y$ will be zero, for agent B will choose his action y to maximize their common utility function $U(x,y)$, and so equations (3.4) and (3.5) will be identical, as will the precommitment and discretionary equilibria.

The assumption of selfish agents matters in so far as the objectives of selfish agents will not perfectly coincide (and this is at least partly what we mean when we say that agents are selfish). It is this imperfect coincidence of objectives, in turn, which makes possible the time-inconsistency of optimal plans, and which makes intelligible the set of social institutions we observe. Altruism is not only not needed to explain the existence of social institutions, but would also make those institutions redundant.

Now, simply saying that people are imperfectly altruistic, so that their objectives do not perfectly coincide, is part, but not all, of what economists mean when they assume rational, self-interested individual behaviour. Though the restrictions are rarely made explicit, not everything is acceptable for positing as an agent's objective, and this is just as well, for otherwise any behaviour could be 'explained' by saying that the agent wanted to behave that way. The sorts of things that would seem particularly unacceptable for simply positing as an agent's objectives are those things whose very existence logically requires human and *a fortiori* social interaction. It is acceptable, for instance, to say that people drink beer because they like beer (even though it may be an acquired taste, and frequently acquired by drinking with others), but it is not acceptable to say that people keep promises and obey laws because they like doing so. This is because things like promises and laws cannot *logically* exist apart from human interaction (whereas beer can logically exist on Mars), and it is human *inter*action that we seek to explain by assuming rational individual behaviour. Economists' explanations of the behaviour of any single individual are indeed no more than abstract, stylised (and so impoverished) redescriptions of common sense explanations. The payoff comes only when the economist (or any other social scientist who shares the individualistic approach) is able to fit these abstract individuals together into a structure of interaction, where one agent's actions are another agent's constraints and vice versa. To posit a taste for keeping promises and obeying the law to explain the institutions of promising and of law is to assume the conclusion. Those institutions, like all institutions, are aspects of human behaviour — namely the following of rules of action by agents who seek thereby to influence other agents' expectations of their future actions.

References

Akerlof, G. A. (1970) 'The Market for "Lemons": Quality uncertainty and the market mechanism', *Quarterly Journal of Economics*, vol. 84, August, pp. 488–500.

Angell, N. (1929) *The Story of Money*, Garden City Publishing Co., New York.

Berger, P. and T. Luckmann (1966) *The Social Construction of Reality: A Treatise in the Sociology of Knowledge*, Doubleday.

Calvo, G. and S. Wellisz (1978) 'Supervision, loss of control, and the optimum size of the firm', *Journal of Political Economy*, vol. 86, October, pp. 943–52.

Coase, R. H. (1960) 'The problem of social cost', *Journal of Law and Economics*, vol. 3, October, pp. 1–45.

Cross, J. G. (1965) 'A theory of the bargaining process', *American Economic Review*, vol. 55, March, pp. 67–94.

Demsetz, H. (1967) 'Towards a theory of property rights', *American Economic Review*, vol. 57, May, pp. 347–59.

Durkheim, E. (1895) *The Rules of Sociological Method*, Free Press, Glencoe, Ill.

Durkheim, E. (1898) 'Individualism and the intellectuals', reprinted in R. N. Bellah (ed.) (1973) *Emile Durkheim on Morality and Society*, University of Chicago Press.

Gintis, H. and S. Bowles (1981) 'Structure and practice in the labor theory of value', *The Review of Radical Political Economics*, vol. 12, no. 4, pp. 1–26.

Grice, H. P. (1969) 'Utterer's meaning and intentions', *Philosophical Review*, vol. 78, April, pp. 147–77.

Hayek, F. A. (1942) 'The facts of the social sciences' in (1969) *Individualism and Economic Order*, Routledge.

Hayek, F. A. (1973) *Law, Legislation and Liberty*, vol. 1, University of Chicago Press.

Hechter, M. (ed) (1983) *The Microfoundations of Macrosociology*, Temple University Press, Philadelphia.

Hicks, J. R. (1964) *The Theory of Wages*, 2nd edn, Macmillan.

Hodgson, D. H. (1967) *The Consequences of Utilitarianism*, Clarendon Press.

Hume, D. (1742) 'Of the balance of trade', in (1963) *Essays, Moral, Political and Literary*, Oxford University Press.

Hume, D. (1777) *An Enquiry Concerning the Principles of Morals*, reprinted in H. D. Aitken (ed) (1968) *Hume's Moral and Political Philosophy*, Hafner, New York.

Kreps, D. M. and R. Wilson (1982a) 'Sequential equilibria', *Econometrica*, vol. 50, no. 4, July, pp. 863–94.

Kreps, D. M. and R. Wilson (1982b), 'Reputation and imperfect information' *Journal of Economic Theory*, vol. 27, no. 2, August, pp. 253–79.

Kydland, F. E. and E. C. Prescott (1977) 'Rules rather than discretion: the inconsistency of optimal plans', *Journal of Political Economy*, vol. 85, June, pp. 473–91.

Macdonald, G. (1984) 'New directions in the economic theory of agency', *Canadian Journal of Economics*, vol. 17, August, pp. 415–40.

Milgrom, P. and J. Roberts (1982) 'Limit pricing and entry under incomplete information: an equilibrium analysis', *Econometrica*, vol. 50, no. 2, March, pp. 443–60.

Nozick, R. (1974) *Anarchy, State and Utopia*, Basic Books.

Okun, A. M. (1981) *Prices and Quantities: A Macroeconomic Analysis*, Brookings Institution.

Patinkin, D. (1965) *Money, Interest and Prices*, 2nd edn, Harper and Row.

Rawls, J. (1971) *A Theory of Justice*, Harvard University Press.

Robbins, L. (1932) *The Nature and Significance of Economic Science*, Macmillan.

Schelling, T. S. (1960) *The Strategy of Conflict*, Harvard University Press.

Schotter, A. (1981) *The Economic Theory of Social Institutions*, Cambridge University Press.

Selten, R. (1975) 'Re-examination of the perfectness concept for equilibrium points in extensive games', *International Journal of Game Theory*, vol. 4, no. 1, pp. 25–55.

Shapiro, C. and J. E. Stiglitz (1984) 'Equilibrium unemployment as a worker discipline device', *American Economic Review*, vo. 74, no. 3, June, pp. 433–44.

Skogh, G. and C. Stuart (1982) 'A contractarian theory of property rights and crime', *Scandinavian Journal of Economics*, vol. 84.

Smith, A. (1776) *The Wealth of Nations*, University of Chicago Press.

Stigler, G. J. (1970) 'The optimum enforcement of laws', *Journal of Political Economy*, vol. 78, no. 3, pp. 526–36.

Thompson, E. A. and R. C. Faith (1981) 'A pure theory of strategic behavior and social institutions', *American Economic Review*, vol. 71, no. 3, June, pp. 366–80.

Turner, J. H. (1978) *The Structure of Sociological Theory*, revised edn, Dorsey Press, Homewood, Ill.
Umbeck, J. (1981), 'Might makes rights: a theory of the foundation and initial distribution of property rights', *Economic Inquiry*, vol. 19, January, pp. 38–59.

Index